FIRST EDITION

STOCK CAR RACING

A Fun, Educational & Interactive
TRIVIA GAMEBOOK

Including Humorous Quotations & Nostalgic Notes

Compiled and written by
Steve McCormick

"Thanks to my Dad, who took me to th

PockitBook Pockit Book™ Publishing

STOCK CAR RACING

TABLE OF GAMES

Copyright logos, trademarks and trade names are the exclusive property of the corporations and organizations of said names, and in no way do they endorse or affiliate with this product, "YaKnow Stock Car Racing Trivia."

DO YOU KNOW WHAT YOU DON'T KNOW?

CORRECTION
REWARD!

YaKnow? Trivia "CORRECTION REWARD"
The first person to prove an incorrect answer to any question in this book will receive one free "YaKnow Trivia" Gamebook of your choice - in stock! Send documentation of corrected answer, with your name, address and phone number, to: Pockitbook Publishing, Inc., P.O. Box 6753, Athens, GA 30604. Thank you.

"YaKnow? Trivia"gamebooks feature fun, interactive and educational trivia games designed to entertain one player or many. Test yourself and friends to see how much yaknow.

Rules & Instructions

THE GAME SET UP: This book contains 50 Trivia Games with 900 questions and answers. There is one game per two pages. Each game's questions are located at the top of one page with its corresponding answers on the page directly below (beneath score card). Each game has three categories, with six questions in each category. Questions 1 and 2 are the easiest; questions 3 and 4 are harder; questions 5 and 6 are the toughest.

KEEPING SCORE: Every correct answer is awarded 1, 2 or 3 points depending on the difficulty of the question in each set. Correct answers to questions 1 or 2 are awarded one point each; 3 or 4 are given two points each; 5 or 6 are given three points each. An incorrect answer does not reduce your score... because trying is encouraged.

| QUESTION | Questions In A Box Earn DOUBLE POINTS

Any Question found with a box outline is a tougher-than-usual question for that set. If answered correctly, that player should earn double the points than normally alloted for the set value.

TO PLAY ALONE: Use the inside flap (connected to the back cover of this book) to hide the answer pages. The Score Box is at the top of each 'Answer Page,' so you don't have to peek to keep your score. Answer the three #1 questions in each category and record your score for each question. Then answer the three #2 questions in each category and so on. Of course, 36 would be a perfect game score.

PLAYING IN A GROUP: Group games are fun, but require a Moderator to read the questions and to keep score. Write the initials or names of each player (Contestant) on the Score Card.

The Moderator selects a category to start. As a question is read, the first Player to say the correct answer aloud gets the point(s) [Note: Game can also be played with first player raising a hand, or knocking on a table, for the right to answer the question]. If a player answers correctly, that player can select the next question or another category. If the answer is wrong, another player can try to answer. If no one guesses correctly, the moderator reads the next (unasked) question, and so on.

You can keep score by simply using dots, slashes or checks for each point earned. Any of these rules may be changed to suit your preferences. That's all there is to it... so, go play and have FUN!

Published by PockitBook Publishing, Inc. – Printed in the U.S.A.

YaKnow?™ STOCK CAR RACING is published by PockitBook Publishing, Inc. located in Athens, GA. All content is considered accurate at time of publication. Any omissions, typographical errors or misprints are unintentional. If error is found, publisher requests documentation for future printings. Copyright logos, trademarks and trade names are the exclusive property of the corporations or organizations of said names.

© 2005, PockitBook Publishing, Inc. All rights reserved. **PockitBook Publishing, Inc.**
P.O. Box 6753
Compiled & Written by Steve McCormick   Athens, GA 30604
-- NASCAR Guide for About.com - www.nascar.about.com   706-354-8380
Edited & Designed by Pete Barkelew   www.yaknowtrivia.com
Printed by Atlanta Web, Atlanta, GA   www.pockitbook.com

Library of Congress Cataloging-in-Publication Data
has been applied for.

                                    Some resources used for statistics and facts:
ISBN 0-9761716-4-3   About.com -- www.nascar.about.com
1. Yaknow? STOCK CAR   NASCAR -- www.nascar.com
   RACING   Racing-Reference.com -- www.racing-reference.com

YaKnow? Trivia Game Books - Patent Pending
YaKnow?™ logo is trademarked by PockitBook Publishing, Inc. All rights reserved.

Daytona 500	Dale Earnhardt	Great Races

1 POINT

Daytona 500

1. While leading in 2002, who got sent to the back of the pack for tugging on his fender during a red flag with 5 laps to go?

2. How many laps is the scheduled distance for the Daytona 500?

Dale Earnhardt

1. After years of trying, Dale Earnhardt finally won the Daytona 500 in what year?

2. At what race track did Dale win his first NASCAR Cup race in. July of 1979?

Great Races

1. The 26th and final regular season race before the first Chase for the Cup was at what track?

2. When Texas Motor Speedway opened in April of 1997, who took the first win there?

2 POINTS

Daytona 500

3. What driver currently holds the record as the youngest Daytona 500 winner ever?

4. In 1978 what driver set the record for the worst starting spot for a Daytona 500 winner?

Dale Earnhardt

3. How many times did Dale win the 'NMPA Most Popular Driver' award when he was driving?*

4. Who was the crew chief for Dale Earnhardt's final Championship in 1994?

Great Races

3. Restrictor plates were used at one track other than at Daytona or Talladega - Where was this unusual race?**

4. In 1980 the final race of the season was the L.A. Times 500 at what track?

3 POINTS

Daytona 500

5. Two drivers share the record for the most career Daytona 500 poles... Cale Yarborough and who else?

6. Who was the first driver to win the Daytona 500 as both a driver and as a car owner?

Dale Earnhardt

5. At what race track did Earnhardt win his first NASCAR Cup pole?

6. Dale Earnhardt won the very first Busch Series race he ever entered. What race track saw him accomplish this feat?

Great Races

5. In a race that lasted over 6 hours, who survived to win the very first Southern 500?

6. When Michigan International Speedway opened in 1969, who won the first NASCAR race held there?

Contestant	Scoring Area	TALLY

Daytona 500	**Dale Earnhardt**	**Great Races**

1-POINT-ANSWERS

Daytona 500	Dale Earnhardt	Great Races
1. Sterling Marlin	1. 1998	1. Richmond International Raceway
2. 200	2. Bristol Motor Speedway	2. Jeff Burton

2-POINT-ANSWERS

Daytona 500	Dale Earnhardt	Great Races
3. Jeff Gordon 25yrs, 6mos, 12days	3. Zero*	3. New Hampshire International Speedway**
4. Bobby Allison (33rd)	4. Andy Petree	4. Ontario Motor Speedway (CA)

3-POINT-ANSWERS

Daytona 500	Dale Earnhardt	Great Races
5. Buddy Baker	5. Riverside International Raceway	5. Johnny Mantz
6. Lee Petty	6. Daytona International Speedway (1982)	6. Cale Yarborough

* Dale Earnhardt only won the Most Popular Driver award one time, after his death in 2001.

** After the deaths of Kenny Irwin and Adam Petty, earlier in 2000, NASCAR felt that they needed to make a safety change for that September's race.

*"God created bumpers and…
bumpers were made for bumping!"*
Dale Earnhardt

Richard Petty	**Race Tracks**	**Racing Teams**

1 POINT

Richard Petty	Race Tracks	Racing Teams
1. In what year did Richard Petty win his final race?	1. Of the 36 points races on the 2004 Cup schedule, how many were on short tracks?*	1. 2004 was the first time someone other than Bill Elliott won a race for Evernham Motorsports - what driver broke the streak?
2. From 1963 to 1977, Petty finished 1-2 63 times with what other hot driver winning 33 of those races to Petty's 30?	2. What track opened in 2001 to see Jeff Gordon win its inaugural NASCAR race?	2. Who was the legendary gasman for Dale Earnhardt's #3?

2 POINTS

Richard Petty	Race Tracks	Racing Teams
3. What crew chief helped Richard Petty win all 7 of his NASCAR Championships?	3. What famous short track hosted its final NASCAR race on September 29, 1996?	3. What former NASCAR crew chief spent the 2004 season as Dale Earnhardt Jr's spotter?
4. Richard learned the business side of the sport after his father was injured in 1961 at what race track?	4. The record for consecutive wins at Infineon Raceway is held by what driver at 3?	4. Mike Rich was a crew member for what driver when he was killed on pit road in 1986?

3 POINTS

Richard Petty	Race Tracks	Racing Teams
5. Richard Petty set the record for most wins in one season when he went on a tear in 1967. How many times did he visit Victory Lane that year?	5. What race track saw 44 cars take the green flag in 1995 and 1996, instead of the normal 43?	5. Who won Championships in 1955 and 1956 as both car owner and crew chief but with two different drivers?
6. What year was Petty Motorsports formed?**	6. What track saw Davey Allison finish 3rd in what would end up being his last NASCAR race ever?	6. Herb Nab lead what driver to back-to-back Championships in the late 70's?

Contestant	Scoring Area	TALLY

Richard Petty	**Race Tracks**	**Racing Teams**

1-POINT-ANSWERS

Richard Petty	Race Tracks	Racing Teams
1. 1984	1. 6*	1. Jeremy Mayfield
2. David Pearson	2. Kansas Speedway	2. Danny "Chocolate" Myers

2-POINT-ANSWERS

Richard Petty	Race Tracks	Racing Teams
3. Dale Inman	3. North Wilkesboro	3. Steve Hmiel
4. Daytona	4. Jeff Gordon	4. Bill Elliott

3-POINT-ANSWERS

Richard Petty	Race Tracks	Racing Teams
5. 27	5. Phoenix International Raceway	5. Carl Kiekhaefer
6. 1949**	6. New Hampshire Intrernational Speedway	6. Cale Yarborough

* Two each at Bristol, Martinsville and Richmond.
** The team was formed by Lee Petty and competed in the team's first race at Charlotte Motor Speedway in July of 1949. Lee scored the team's first win just 5 races later at Heidelberg Speedway in PA.

"The good Lord doesn't tell you what His plan is, so all you can do is get up in the morning and see what happens next."
-- Richard Petty

"Drivin' a race car is like dancing with a chain saw."
-- Cale Yarborough

9

	Champions	**Racing Families**	**History**
1 POINT	1. What driver won 11 races in 1985, but didn't win a Championship until 3 years later?	1. Which Burton brother was first to score a win at Daytona International Speedway?	1. What track sparked controversy and a driver boycott when it opened in 1969?
	2. What year did Dale Jarrett claim his NASCAR Cup title?	2. What third-generation driver won his very first start, an ARCA race at Daytona in 1979?	2. The Modern Era of NASCAR began in what year when the schedule was trimmed from 48 races to 31?
2 POINTS	3. How many NEXTEL Cup Titles did Darrell Waltrip win?	3. Father and son Buddy and Todd Parrott are both excellent NASCAR Cup crew chiefs, but which one has a Championship?	3. In 1950 what driver would have won his first title if not for being penalized 809 points for racing in non-NASCAR events?
	4. The second of two consecutive championships was the one that made what driver the first to earn one million dollars in one season?	4. Who are the only two brothers to have each won the Daytona 500?	4. Bill France Sr. was born in what American city?
3 POINTS	5. In 1970, Harry Hyde led what driver to his only NASCAR Championship?	5. The Alabama Gang was founded by Red Farmer and what two brothers?	5. NASCAR's very first Cup race began with controversy as what driver crossed the finish line first only to be disqualified later?
	6. Earning more than twice the money of the previous champion, who was the first to win more than $100,000 in one season?	6. What racing family started out building cars for Marty Robbins and today their 3rd and 4th generation are driving them?*	6. What year was the first night race held in Bristol?**

Contestant	Scoring Area	TALLY

Champions	**Racing Families**	**History**

1-POINT-ANSWERS

Champions	**Racing Families**	**History**
1. Bill Elliott	1. Jeff (July 2000)	1. Talladega Superspeedway
2. 1999	2. Kyle Petty	2. 1972

2-POINT-ANSWERS

Champions	**Racing Families**	**History**
3. Three - '81, '82 & '85	3. Son Todd (Dale Jarrett 1999)	3. Lee Petty
4. Dale Earnhardt	4. Darrell and Michael Waltrip	4. Washington DC

3-POINT-ANSWERS

Champions	**Racing Families**	**History**
5. Bobby Isaac	5. Bobby and Donnie Allison	5. Glenn Dunnaway
6. Richard Petty (1964)	6. Hamiltons*	6. 1978**

* Bobby Hamilton Sr's father and great grandfather built cars. Now Bobby and his son Bobby Jr. are top tier racers
** Cale Yarborough won the race that day in an Oldsmobile with an average speed of 88.628 MPH.

"I keep trying to get Junior to come back to the track and help me. I asked him at Bristol, 'Junior, just come over and stand in the pits with a headset on the wall like you used to.' And he said, 'Boy, you ain't running good enough for me to help you.'" -- Darrell Waltrip, when he was owner/driver

"I thought maybe he needed a psychologist, first off for owning a race team and secondly for hiring me."
-- Bill Elliott on Ray Evernham

11

Racing Technology	Nicknames	Racing Sponsors
1 POINT		
1. The person from each team who watches from high above and talks to the driver is referred to as...?	1. 'The Ironman' has been used to describe a number of drivers through the years, but only one of them was also 'The Iceman.'	1. Before Kyle Busch carried the Kellogg's colors in 2005, what other driver had success for that sponsor?
2. What is the thin piece of metal put between the carb and the manifold to limit speed?	2. Which track claims to be 'The World's Fastest Half-Mile'?	2. It should come as no surprise that what beverage is the official beer of NASCAR?
2 POINTS		
3. What company created NASCAR's tire wars in 1994 when they entered NASCAR with Geoff Bodine?	3. Which NASCAR Cup venue refers to itself modestly as the 'World Center of Racing'?	3. The traditional Southern 500 Labor Day race in Darlington ended its run in 2004 sponsored by what brand?
4. What is the minimum weight allowed for a race-ready NEXTEL Cup race car without the driver?	4. Sterling Marlin's father, also a NASCAR racer, was much better known by what nickname?	4. Winston is a brand name belonging to what major corporation?*
3 POINTS		
5. What is the term that describes the difference in circumference between the left and right side tires?**	5. This driver was known as 'One Tough Customer' because of his sponsor before he moved on to better known nicknames.	5. When Terry Labonte won the 1984 Championship who was the sponsor on his #44 car?
6. In 1952 what electronic devices made their first appearance in NASCAR?	6. Who drove a car called 'The Underbird' when he clinch a NASCAR title?	6. Who was the sponsor of Rusty Wallace's 1989 Championship winning team?

Contestant	Scoring Area	TALLY

Racing Technology	**Nicknames**	**Racing Sponsors**

1-POINT-ANSWERS

1. Spotter	1. Terry Labonte	1. Terry Labonte
2. Restrictor Plate	2. Bristol Motor Speedway	2. Budweiser

2-POINT-ANSWERS

3. Hoosier	3. Daytona International Speedway	3. Mountain Dew
4. 3,400 pounds	4. Coo Coo	4. RJ Reynolds*

3-POINT-ANSWERS

5. Stagger**	5. Dale Earnhardt	5. Piedmont Airlines
6. Two-way driver radios	6. Alan Kulwicki	6. Kodiak

* They were also known as RJR Nabisco until Nabisco spun off in 1999. Then in July 2004, they merged with another tobacco company and changed their name to Reynolds American Inc.
** Stagger was more important in the era of biased-ply tires. With the introduction of radial tires stagger has reduced importance.

"We had the wrong gear, wrong springs, wrong shocks and wrong car. We had the right beer, but other than that, we got stomped." -- Sterling Marlin (Coors Lite)

"I'll apologize to them after they get me to the front!"
-- Dale Earnhardt (after his crew chief said he was hurting his tires and needed to conserve them)

Drivers	Manufacturers	Rookies

1 POINT

Drivers

1. Who is the only driver to win four NASCAR Cup races in a row at Talladega?

2. What driver won 10 consecutive 'Most Popular Driver' awards, from 1991 through 2000?

Manufacturers

1. Which car maker can boast that it provides the official pace car of NASCAR?

2. What former crew chief left his Championship team to lead the Dodge return to NASCAR in 2001?

Rookies

1. Kyle Busch raced for the 2005 NASCAR Cup 'Rookie of the Year' honors for what car owner?

2. What driver beat Jimmie Johnson for 'Rookie of the Year' honors in 2002?

2 POINTS

Drivers

3. Though he raced for 8 more years what driver scored the final win of his hall of fame career at the 1992 Southern 500?

4. Who is the only African-American to ever win a NASCAR race?*

Manufacturers

3. In 1953 Oldsmobile, Lincoln and Hudson introduced what to try to limit breakage?**

4. What manufacturer won their last race in 1990 with Brett Bodine behind the wheel?

Rookies

3. How many of a rookie driver's best finishes are counted towards the Rookie standings?

4. The final points toward the rookie honors are awarded by a panel that includes what other driver?

3 POINTS

Drivers

5. Geoffrey Bodine only has one career race track sweep. It came in 1990 at what speedway?

6. From September 1970 through February 1975 what driver won 9 out of 10 races in Richmond?

Manufacturers

5. What year did Oldsmobile last win the NEXTEL Cup manufacturers title?

6. Lee Petty brought Chrysler its first NASCAR NEXTEL Cup Championship in what year?

Rookies

5. In 1985 what current NASCAR NEXTEL Cup driver won the Rookie of the Year title?

6. NASCAR first honored its Rookie of the Year in 1958. What driver won the rookie title then?

Contestant	Scoring Area	TALLY

Drivers	**Manufacturers**	**Rookies**
1-POINT-ANSWERS		
1. Dale Earnhardt Jr.	1. Chevrolet (Monte Carlo)	1. Rick Hendrick
2. Bill Elliott	2. Ray Evernham	2. Ryan Newman
2-POINT-ANSWERS		
3. Darrell Waltrip	3. "Severe Usage Kits" **	3. 17
4. Wendell Scott*	4. Buick	4. The defending NASCAR Champion
3-POINT-ANSWERS		
5. Martinsville Speedway	5. 1978	5. Ken Schrader
6. Richard Petty	6. 1954	6. Shorty Rollins

* Scott won a race in Jacksonville, Florida in 1963. He was not originally awarded the win but after a scoring review it was decided that he had, in fact, won.

** These kits included beefier suspension parts, spindles hubs and axles.

"If your car is running bad, then it's about as fun as a root canal." -- Ken Schrader

"Those boys playing football get their $2 or $3 million up front, and if they don't have a good day, they are not out anything. They still get paid on Monday. If we don't win, we don't get paid on Monday." -- Richard Petty (before NASCAR starting making and paying the big bucks)

15

Racing Teams	Daytona 500	Racing Rules
1 POINT		
1. Who was the crew chief for Jeff Gordon's 1991 NASCAR Cup title?	1. In 2001, what driver won the race while the Dale Earnhardt tragedy unfolded behind him in turn 4?	1. As of the middle of the 2003 season, drivers can no longer do what when the yellow flag comes out?
2. After many years in NASCAR Jimmy Fennig was crew chief for what NEXTEL Cup Champion?	2. What year did Dale Earnhardt finally get his long sought Daytona 500 victory?	2. On a restart, all passing must be done to which side until you cross the line?
2 POINTS		
3. Who was the first driver that Robert Yates Racing ever hired?	3. The first points race after the Y2K scare was the 2000 Daytona 500 which was won by what driver?	3. What driver holds the record for the largest monetary fine in NASCAR history?*
4. Who was Cale Yarborough's car owner when he clicked off three consecutive NEXTEL Cup titles in the 70s?	4. Which manufacturer won the Daytona 500 more recenty Buick or Pontiac?	4. What does NASCAR do with all money collected from fines during the season?
3 POINTS		
5. What driver brought Roger Penske his first victory as a car owner when he won at Riverside?	5. What crossover racing star made his only NEXTEL Cup start driving for Hendrick in the 1993 Daytona 500?	5. If a driver ignores the black flag for too long what flag will they see which means they are no longer being scored?
6. Who was the last driver to win the Championship while also acting as his own crew chief?	6. David Pearson scored his only Daytona 500 victory while driving what make of car?	6. NEXTEL Cup engine compression is limited to no more than what ratio?

Contestant	Scoring Area	TALLY

Racing Teams	Daytona 500	Racing Rules

1-POINT-ANSWERS

Racing Teams	Daytona 500	Racing Rules
1. Robbie Loomis	1. Michael Waltrip	1. Race back to the line (Pass)
2. Kurt Busch	2. 1998	2. Right

2-POINT-ANSWERS

Racing Teams	Daytona 500	Racing Rules
3. Davey Allison	3. Dale Jarrett	3. Jeff Gordon*
4. Junior Johnson	4. Buick	4. It is added to the year-end points fund

3-POINT-ANSWERS

Racing Teams	Daytona 500	Racing Rules
5. Mark Donohue	5. Al Unser Jr.	5. Black with a white X
6. Lee Petty	6. Mercury	6. 12:0

* At Lowes Motor Speedway in May of 1995 Jeff Gordon was fined $60,000 for unapproved suspension parts.

"I just couldn't wait 'til I got that big grab on the neck, that big hug. I just knew, any minute, Dale was going to join me in Victory Lane, and say, 'That's what I'm talking about, right there!' That wasn't to be. My belief is in a twinkle of an eye... you're in the presence of the Lord. And that's where I think Dale is." -- Michael Waltrip, after winning the 2001 Daytona 500.

"With two laps to go then the action will begin, unless this is the action, which it is." -- Murray Walker

"It's the big Daytona. It's kind of like a roller coaster."
-- Brian Vickers, referring to the Daytona 500

	History	Coca-Cola 600	Race Tracks
1 POINT	1. The very first NASCAR sanctioned event was a 150-mile modified race at what track?	1. What driver currently holds the record for the most Coca-Cola 600 victories with 5?	1. What is the name of the lake in the infield at Daytona International Speedway?
	2. What race track held the first NASCAR Cup race on an all-concrete surface?	2. The fastest Coca-Cola 600 in history was in 1995 when what driver averaged 151.952mph?	2. What Kansas race track hosted Truck Series road racing from 1995 through 1999?
2 POINTS	3. What did Richard Nixon do in 1970 that altered the course of NASCAR history?*	3. What year did the total purse for the Coca-Cola 600 first surpass $1,000,000?	3. Kevin Harvick won what track's very first Cup race when it opened in 2001?
	4. NASCAR's first strictly stock race was held on what three-quarter mile dirt oval?	4. The first back-to-back Coca-Cola 600 winner came in 1972 and 1973 when what driver dominated?	4. In 1997 what driver won the inaugural NEXTEL Cup race at California Speedway?
3 POINTS	5. What year did Bill France Sr. first promote a race on the beach/road course in Daytona?	5. What driver was the last Pontiac driver to win the Coca-Cola 600 when he won the 1990 event?	5. In 1969, the two Cup races in Michigan were scheduled to run how many miles combined?**
	6. What track was the farthest north that the Cup drivers raced on during the 1949 season?	6. Who became the first two-time winner of the Coca-Cola 600 when he won the 1963 and 1965 events?	6. What driver won the first Busch race ever held at Phoenix International Raceway in 1999?

Contestant	Scoring Area	TALLY

History	**Coca-Cola 600**	**Race Tracks**

1-POINT-ANSWERS

History	Coca-Cola 600	Race Tracks
1. Daytona Beach/ Road Course	1. Darrell Waltrip	1. Lake Lloyd
2. Bristol Motor Speedway	2. Bobby Labonte	2. Heartland Park Topeka

2-POINT-ANSWERS

History	Coca-Cola 600	Race Tracks
3. Banned cigarette advertising from TV and Radio*	3. 1994	3. Chicagoland Speedway
4. Charlotte Speedway	4. Buddy Baker	4. Jeff Gordon

3-POINT-ANSWERS

History	Coca-Cola 600	Race Tracks
5. 1937	5. Rusty Wallace	5. 1100**
6. Hamburg Speedway (NY)	6. Fred Lorenzen	6. Jeff Gordon

* This forced cigarette manufacturers like RJ Reynolds to seek alternative advertising venues. In 1971, the Winston Cup series was born.

** The June race ran the fully scheduled 500 miles while the August 600 miler was shortened by rain to 330 miles.

"It's not a pretty sight watching a dot behind you get really big all of a sudden." -- Tony Stewart, after the Pepsi 400 at Daytona

"Track position isn't everything, but it's a good start." -- Ryan Newman, who won nine poles

19

Jeff Gordon	Great Races	Brickyard 400

1 POINT

1. Jeff Gordon scored 7 wins on his way to his first NEXTEL Cup Championship in what year?

1. In 1987, what driver set the all-time stock car speed record when he ran 212.809 mph at Talladega?

1. What driver scored Pontiac's only Brickyard 400 victory when he took the checkers in 2000?

2. At what race track did Jeff Gordon make his NASCAR Cup debut?

2. In 2001, Kevin Harvick scored his first victory in an emotional win at what race track?

2. The Brickyard 400 is scheduled to run how many laps?

2 POINTS

3. What year did Jeff Gordon first crack one million dollars in single-season earnings?

3. What race track saw Joe Nemechek score his first NEXTEL Cup victory during the 1999 season?

3. What driver sat on the pole in 1995 and again in 1996 to become the first 2-time Brickyard pole sitter?

4. What car number did Jeff drive during his two full Busch series campaigns?

4. What driver did Kevin Harvick nip by just .006 seconds to score his first Cup win in 2001?

4. Who is the only owner-driver to win the Brickyard 400?

3 POINTS

5. Jeff tied the record for modern era wins in a single season in what year?

5. In 1965, Ned Jarrett layed down one of the most dominating performances of all time when he won by 14 laps at what track?

5. Of the three Bodine brothers who started the inaugural Brickyard 400, who had the best finish?

6. What stock car owner first put Jeff Gordon and Ray Evernham together?

6. What year did NASCAR first race in Suzuka, Japan?

6. What year was the fastest Brickyard 400, with only one caution and a 155.206 mph avg speed?

Contestant	Scoring Area	TALLY

Jeff Gordon	**Great Races**	**Brickyard 400**
1-POINT-ANSWERS		
1. 1995	1. Bill Elliott	1. Bobby Labonte
2. Atlanta Motor Speedway	2. Atlanta Motor Speedway	2. 160
2-POINT-ANSWERS		
3. 1994	3. New Hampshire International Speedway	3. Jeff Gordon
4. #1	4. Jeff Gordon	4. Ricky Rudd
3-POINT-ANSWERS		
5. 1998	5. Darlington Raceway	5. Brett (2nd)
6. Bill Davis	6. 1996	6. 1995

"When you pull into victory lane, it makes you feel good that you just ruined their day." -- Jeff Gordon commenting on all of the anti-Gordon fan displays

"At this point, I think if I saw someone on the side of the road selling horseshoes, I would stop and buy one." -- Bobby Labonte, in the midst of a tough season

"NASCAR couldn't run a legitimate business if there was a teacher's pet." -- Dale Earnhardt Jr.

"I love this old track. It's a neat place. Got good hot dogs, too." -- Sterling Marlin, on Martinsville.

Race Tracks	Champions	Nicknames

1 POINT

Race Tracks	Champions	Nicknames
1. NASCAR first visited this track in 1953 when it was a half-mile dirt oval. In 2004, what track is now a 3/4 mile paved D?	1. In 1994, Rockingham was the site where what driver clinched the Championship?	1. 'The King' can only refer to one NASCAR legend... who was he?
2. What challenging track measures exactly 1.366 miles?	2. Who was the last driver to win a championship with a team that he also owned?	2. This legendary race track leads the league in colorful nicknames, but most know her simply as 'The Lady In Black.'

2 POINTS

Race Tracks	Champions	Nicknames
3. The NASCAR drivers visited what California track annually from 1971 through 1980?	3. Who was the first driver to ever win both the Busch series and NASCAR Cup Championships?	3. What was Glenn Roberts' nickname that he claimed followed him to racing from his baseball days?
4. In 1999, what race track hosted a NASCAR Cup race for the first time?	4. Name any one of the three tracks Tony Stewart won at during his Championship winning season.	4. What occasionally reckless driver earned the nickname 'Swervin'' the hard way?

3 POINTS

Race Tracks	Champions	Nicknames
5. From 1953-71, what N.C. track hosted Cup racing and then returned from 1982-98 to host the Busch series on its .363 mile oval?	5. As America celebrated her bicentennial in 1976, what driver celebrated his first, but not last, Championship?	5. Known as 'The Hat Man,' this famous NASCAR face coordinated the Victory Lane ceremonies for Unocal 76 for years.
6. Who has the most poles at Bristol?	6. Four drivers have won Most Popular and the Championship in the same year, name two.	6. What driver is called "Herman" from comic book character "Herman the German?"

Contestant	Scoring Area	TALLY

Race Tracks   Champions   Nicknames

1-POINT-ANSWERS

Race Tracks	Champions	Nicknames
1. Richmond International Raceway	1. Dale Earnhardt	1. Richard Petty
2. Darlington Raceway	2. Alan Kulwicki	2. Darlington Raceway

2-POINT-ANSWERS

Race Tracks	Champions	Nicknames
3. Ontario Motor Speedway (CA)	3. Bobby Labonte	3. 'Fireball'
4. Homestead-Miami Speedway	4. Atlanta, Richmond and Watkins Glen	4. Ernie Irvan

3-POINT-ANSWERS

Race Tracks	Champions	Nicknames
5. Hickory Speedway	5. Cale Yarborough	5. Bill Brodrick
6. Cale Yarborough	6. Rex White, Richard Petty, Bobby Allison and Bill Elliott	6. Kenny Wallace

---

"How tough is Darlington? Well, Richard Petty won one Southern 500. That should tell you something." -- Kyle Petty

"The new asphalt is like putting a tuxedo on a rattlesnake." -- Buddy Baker, referring to Darlington Raceway

"Short track racing is by all means a contact sport." -- Buddy Baker, From Hickory Speedway

"Cale Yarborough would wear out a set of gloves a race pulling them up." -- Buddy Baker

Families	Teams	Drivers

1 POINT

Families
1. Of the three Bodine brothers, who have all raced in NASCAR, which one has the most wins?

2. Drivers with what last name have won more NASCAR races than any other?*

Teams
1. When Bobby Labonte won the NASCAR Cup title, who was his crew chief?

2. Bill Elliott brought what car owner his first win in 2001, when he won from the pole in Homestead?

Drivers
1. Who was the first NASCAR driver to earn more than $1million in his career?**

2. What driver scored his first NASCAR Cup victory at Texas Motor Speedway in 2000?

2 POINTS

Families
3. NASCAR driver, Patty Moise, married what former Busch Series regular?

4. Siblings Robin & Ryan Pemberton both made it into NASCAR's top series as crew chief. Which one is the older brother?

Teams
3. What crew chief helped bring Dale Earnhardt his long-sought Daytona 500 victory?

4. The Wood Brothers struck gold in 1973 when what driver brought them 11 wins in only 18 starts?

Drivers
3. Darrell Waltrip is tied for third in all-time series wins with 84. Who is he tied with?

4. Who was the last driver to sweep both Cup races in Darlington when he did it in 1999?

3 POINTS

Families
5. What older sibling of a successful Cup driver won Busch series 'Rookie' honors in 1993?

6. What family has over 1,000 combined NASCAR Cup starts, but all 55 victories are by the same driver?

Teams
5. Who was the owner of the last single-car team to win the NASCAR Cup title? †

6. What year did the legendary Wood Brothers first enter a car in NASCAR's premier racing division?

Drivers
5. In 1981, what driver, with over 500 NASCAR Cup starts, scored his first win at Martinsville?

6. Geoffrey Bodine scored his last NASCAR Cup victory in 1996 at what race track?

Contestant	Scoring Area	TALLY

Families	**Teams**	**Drivers**

1-POINT-ANSWERS

Families	Teams	Drivers
1. Geoffrey (18)	1. Jimmy Makar	1. Richard Petty**
2. Petty*	2. Ray Evernham	2. Dale Earnhardt Jr.

2-POINT-ANSWERS

Families	Teams	Drivers
3. Elton Sawyer	3. Larry McReynolds	3. Bobby Allison
4. Robin (13 years older)	4. David Pearson	4. Jeff Burton

3-POINT-ANSWERS

Families	Teams	Drivers
5. Hermie Sadler	5. Richard Childress†	5. Morgan Shepherd
6. Wallace	6. 1953	6. Watkins Glen

* With 262 wins and 10 NASCAR Championships through three generations, the Pettys are by far the winningest NASCAR family.

** Petty broke through the million mark at the Dixie 500 in Atlanta on August 1, 1971.

† Although Childress would eventually run a multi-car operation, Dale Earnhardt's 1994 title was as a single-car team.

"Junior has gotten to that point where he reminds me a lot of his dad." -- Jeff Gordon, referring to Dale Earnhardt Jr.

"I watched the Masters, and when Phil Mickelson made that putt and everyone had been asking him when he was going to finally win a big one, I turned to my wife and said, 'Well, maybe it's my turn.'" -- Rusty Wallace, after ending a long losing streat at Martinsville.

Busch Series	Richard Petty	Racing Technology
1 POINT		
1. What NASCAR Cup star is part owner of the 2004 Busch Series Championship winning team?	1. Richard Petty said farewell to the driver's seat at Atlanta in November of what year?	1. Michael Waltrip made what safety innovation famous when he used it to celebrate his 2003 Talladega victory?*
2. The 2001 Busch series Championship was claimed by what very busy driver?	2. Richard is the only NASCAR driver to have a color named after him. "Petty" is a shade of what?	2. What is a set of tires that have never been run on before called?
2 POINTS		
3. In 1991, what future NEXTEL Cup star won the Busch series 'Rookie of the Year' honors?	3. Petty's most recent win as a car owner came when what driver won Martinsville in April of 1999?	3. What is the two word phrase that describes the part of the tire that is touching the track?
4. What northerner won 'Most Popular Driver' in the 1997 Busch series?	4. Richard Petty appeared on the Cheerios box for the very first time in what year?**	4. What safety device was mandated in 1988 at Daytona and Talladega beginning with the 500?
3 POINTS		
5. Who won the 1989 Busch series title before having his career cut tragically short the following year?	5. Richard scored his first win at Lowes Motor Speedway when he swept both races in what year?	5. In 1957, what manufacturer pioneered finned aluminum brake drums to reduce heat?
6. Talladega first hosted the Busch series in 1992 when what driver took the win?	6. Petty won 196 races for Petty Enterprises and 2 each for two other car owners. Name either of them.	6. What year did Chevrolet introduce the 355ci small-block V8 to NASCAR?

Contestant	Scoring Area	TALLY

Busch Series	**Richard Petty**	**Racing Technology**

1-POINT-ANSWERS

1. Dale Earnhardt Jr.	1. 1992	1. Roof escape hatch*
2. Kevin Harvick	2. Blue	2. Stickers

2-POINT-ANSWERS

3. Jeff Gordon	3. John Andretti	3. Contact Patch
4. Mike McLaughlin	4. 2000**	4. Restrictor Plate

3-POINT-ANSWERS

5. Rob Moroso	5. 1975	5. Buick
6. Ernie Irvan	6. Don Robertson and Mike Curb	6. 1955

* Michael pulled up on the front stretch in front of the fans and
  popped out of the top of the car.
** This was the year that Cheerios took over for STP on the #43.
  The Pepsi 400 in Daytona was the first race for Cheerios.

*"You've got to have a lead dog. You've got to have somebody
out there for everybody to shoot at."* -- Richard Petty

*"As I walk into the track, I look at the huge banking and
think, 'Why do I like this place so much?' Simple. It's a
driver's dream."* -- Busch Series driver David Green, on
Bristol Motor Speedway

*"This is the only time that you have 50 drivers tied for the
points lead."* -- Benny Parsons on the start of each season

Racing Sponsors	Racing Rules	Dale Earnhardt
1 POINT 1. Bobby Hamilton won the Craftsman Truck Series 2004 Championship with what sponsor on his truck?	1. At Daytona and Talladega, drivers can drive out of bounds as long as they don't do what?	1. What are Dale Earnhardt's children's names?
2. What company was the official fuel of NASCAR until SUNOCO took over that honor in 2004?	2. What color flag does NASCAR display to indicate that there is one lap left in the race?	2. In what non-points race was Dale Earnhardt undefeated for the entire decade of the 90s?
2 POINTS 3. What driver spent the 2004 NEXTEL Cup season driving the #41 Target Dodge?	3. How many drivers are guaranteed a starting position based on their car owner points?*	3. Dale Earnhardt won the NASCAR NEXTEL Cup seven times. Name 6 of those 7 years?
4. Bill Elliott set out on his own as an owner/driver from 1995 until 2001 with what major sponsor?	4. In 2005, NASCAR started mandating what in an effort to limit engine RPM?	4. In his entire NASCAR Cup career, which was better - Earnhardt's average start or his average finish?**
3 POINTS 5. Darrell Waltrip had what primary sponsor on his car when he won 12 races in both 1981 and 1982?	5. If a driver swears on TV, he is penalized under Section 12-4-A of the rulebook which covers actions that are what?	5. Dale Earnhardt's father passed away while working on his own race car in what year?
6. What driver won the Championship the year Winston entered NASCAR in 1971?	6. An appeal of a NASCAR penalty is heard by what body?	6. Dale Earnhardt drove his first race for Richard Childress Racing in what year?

Contestant	Scoring Area	TALLY

Racing Sponsors	Racing Rules	Dale Earnhardt
1-POINT-ANSWERS		
1. Square D	1. Advance their position	1. Kerry, Kelley, Dale Jr., Taylor
2. Unocal (76)	2. White	2. Gatorade Twin 125-mile Daytona 500 qualifying races
2-POINT-ANSWERS		
3. Casey Mears	3. 35*	3. 1980, 1986, 1987, 1990, 1991, 1993, 1994
4. McDonalds	4. Gear ratios	4. Average finish**
3-POINT-ANSWERS		
5. Mountain Dew	5. Actions detrimental to stock car racing	5. 1973
6. Richard Petty	6. National Stock Car Racing Commission	6. 1981

* The top 35 in car owner points are guaranteed a starting spot.
  The remaining 8 positions are filled based on qualifying speed.
** Dale's average finish of 11.1 was better than his 12.9 average
   starting spot.

*"We should have tuned on the bumpers or the rubbers
or the springs or something a little more.
It sure wasn't a good ride."* -- Dale Earnhardt

	Great Races	TV, Movies & Media	History
1 POINT	1. At Texas Motor Speedway in 2000, what driver scored his first Cup series win in only his 12th start? 2. What sitting president was Grand Marshal of Richard Petty's final NASCAR race win?*	1. What Fox broadcast booth member made his name in NASCAR as Davey Allison's crew chief in 1991 and 1992? 2. The 1982 stock car film, 'Six Pack,' featured what musical crossover star?	1. From 1950 until major sponsorship came into the sport after the 1970 season what was NASCAR's top series called? 2. What does the famous acronym NASCAR stand for?
2 POINTS	3. He was practically ignored when he won Homestead in 2004 with the Chase for the Cup raging behind him. 4. The final race in North Wilkesboro was won by what driver in 1996?	3. What network first brought live flag-to-flag television coverage of the Daytona 500 into U.S. homes? 4. What "Days of Thunder" costar later became Tom Cruise's wife?	3. July 31st, 1960 was opening day for the seventh superspeedway in NASCAR history. What track is this? 4. How many divisions were originally created within NASCAR?†
3 POINTS	5. Darrell Waltrip and Richard Petty swapped the lead multiple times in the last few laps of the 1979 Rebel 500. Who won? 6. How many drivers have won both the Daytona 500 and the Indy 500?	5. What TV play-by-play man is credited with naming the Daytona 500 "The Great American Race?" 6. What was the lead character's name in the 1982 film 'Six Pack'?	5. In 1949 Curtis Turner took home the largest winning purse of the year when he won $2,250 at what PA race track? 6. Who sat on the pole for NASCAR's first ever Cup race?

Contestant	Scoring Area	TALLY

	TV, Movies	
Great Races	**& Media**	**History**

1-POINT-ANSWERS

Great Races	TV, Movies & Media	History
1. Dale Earnhardt Jr.	1. Larry McReynolds	1. Grand National
2. Ronald Reagan*	2. Kenny Rogers	2. National Assoc. For Stock Car Auto Racing

2-POINT-ANSWERS

Great Races	TV, Movies & Media	History
3. Greg Biffle	3. CBS	3. Atlanta Motor Speedway
4. Jeff Gordon	4. Nicole Kidman	4. 3 †

3-POINT-ANSWERS

Great Races	TV, Movies & Media	History
5. Darrell Waltrip	5. Ken Squire	5. Langhorne Speedway
6. 2 - AJ Foyt and Mario Andretti	6. Brewster Baker	6. Bob Flock

* This race was on July 4th of 1984 and made for one of the most famous video clips of the year.

† Originally Bill France Sr. wanted to run Modifieds (the primary division in 1948), Roadsters (popular in the north) and Strictly Stock (which eventually became NEXTEL Cup)

"There's no bigger surprise than to be tooling along at 200 mph and suddenly getting hit from the rear."
  -- Darrell Waltrip

"We're having chassis, aero and motor problems. Other than that, things are great." -- Ward Burton

"Drivin' a race car is like dancing with a chain saw."
  -- Cale Yarborough

Rookies	Manufacturers	Race Tracks
1 POINT		
1. How many races can a NEXTEL Cup driver run without losing his Rookie status?	1. What manufacturer pulled out of NASCAR competition after the completion of the 2003 season?	1. Infineon Raceway in California was known by what name before Infineon bought the naming rights?
2. What driver won the truck series Rookie title for rookie manufacturer Toyota?	2. What car maker holds the record for consecutive NASCAR championships with six in a row?*	2. What track is listed at exactly .533 miles in length?
2 POINTS		
3. Who is the only driver in history to win 'Rookie of the Year' and a Championship in consecutive years?	3. In 1992, what car maker won the first 9 races on its way to a runaway manufacturers championship?	3. Only one NEXTEL Cup race has has ever been held in Wisconsin, what race track hosted this event?
4. What year did Tony Stewart win the NASCAR Cup 'Rookie of the Year' honors?	4. In 2004 what driver gave Toyota their first Truck Series Victory?	4. What was the only track to make its NEXTEL Cup debut in 1998?
3 POINTS		
5. Who is the only driver to have won both the Truck and Busch series Rookie titles?	5. In 1961 and '62, what manufacturer set a record for wins by its cars over two consecutive seasons with 52 victories?	5. What Tennessee .596 mile track hosted Cup racing from 1958 until it was taken off the schedule following the 1984 season?
6. In 1997 and 1998, what driver won the Truck and NASCAR Cup series Rookie honors back to back?	6. What car maker won the first NASCAR Championship?	6. What track first made its way onto the Cup schedule in 1974?

Contestant	Scoring Area	TALLY

Rookies	**Manufacturers**	**Race Tracks**

1-POINT-ANSWERS

Rookies	Manufacturers	Race Tracks
1. Seven	1. Pontiac	1. Sears Point Raceway
2. David Reutimann	2. Chevrolet*	2. Bristol Motor Speedway

2-POINT-ANSWERS

Rookies	Manufacturers	Race Tracks
3. Dale Earnhardt - 1979 & 1980	3. Ford	3. Road America - 1956
4. 1999	4. Travis Kvapil	4. Las Vegas Motor Speedway

3-POINT-ANSWERS

Rookies	Manufacturers	Race Tracks
5. Greg Biffle	5. Pontiac	5. Nashville (Fairgrounds) Speedway
6. Kenny Irwin Jr.	6. Oldsmobile	6. Pocono Raceway

* The record setting streak ran from Dale Earnhardt's title in 1993 through Jeff Gordon's championship in 1998

"I would like to thank everbody... you know who you are and your last names." -- Ward Burton, after winning Louden 300

"I never dreamed I would see the sport where it is today. But I did see that when television got into it, there would be no end to where it could go. With television, you could get into everybody's house. People that had never been to a race could see it on television, and then after they went to a race, they're hooked." -- Rex White

Daytona 500	All-Star Race	Coca-Cola 600

1 POINT

1. What driver did the 'Icky Shuffle' in Victory Lane when he finally scored his first Daytona 500?

2. Robert Yates Racing won the 1992 Daytona 500 with what driver behind the wheel?

1. Matt Kenseth was the first driver to win $1 million from the All-Star event when he won in what year?

2. What driver won the 2000 All-Star event in his rookie year?

1. Who won the Coca-Cola 600 and the October race to sweep Lowes Motor Speedway in 2004?

2. In 2002, what driver claimed a Winston No-Bull $1 million bonus when he won the 600?

2 POINTS

3. Who was the first woman to ever start the Daytona 500?*

4. When Lee Petty won his first Daytona 500, what car number did he carry that was later used by others in his family?

3. Dale Earnhardt drove a special red, white and blue Olympic paint scheme in what year's All-Star event?

4. In 1986, the All-Star race was not in Charlotte, but where instead?

3. In 1988 and 1989, what driver won back-to-back Coca-Cola 600s?

4. 1970 saw the most successful double when what driver won the 600 and finished 4th in the 500 in the same year?**

3 POINTS

5. Buddy Baker set the current record for the fastest Daytona 500 in history with an average speed of 177.602 MPH in what year?

6. Who was the last Pontiac driver to win the Daytona 500?

5. Who was the first driver to win the All-Star race on his way to that year's NASCAR Championship?

6. Jeff Gordon was leading in 1998 when he ran out of gas and handed the win to what driver?

5. What driver holds the record for the slowest pole speed in 600 history when he took the starting spot in 1961?

6. What driver pocketed over $27,000 for winning the very first Coca-Cola 600?

Contestant	Scoring Area	TALLY

Daytona 500	All-Star Race	Coca-Cola 600

1-POINT-ANSWERS

1. Darrell Waltrip	1. 2004	1. Jimmie Johnson
2. Davey Allison	2. Dale Earnhardt Jr.	2. Mark Martin

2-POINT-ANSWERS

3. Janet Guthrie*	3. 1996	3. Darrell Waltrip
4. 42	4. Atlanta Motor Speedway	4. Donnie Allison**

3-POINT-ANSWERS

5. Buddy Baker	5. Darrell Waltrip	5. Richard Petty
6. Cale Yarborough	6. Mark Martin	6. Joe Lee Johnson

* Janet had a solid day and finished 12th.
** In 1970, the two races were 6 days apart.

Quotes About Janet Guthrie

"There is no question about her ability to race with us. More power to her. She has 'made it' in what I think is the most competitive racing circuit in the world." -- Cale Yarborough

"If she had a better ride, she'd probably win one of these [Winston Cup] events." -- Richard Petty

"She's done a good job. I gotta admit that I had my doubts about her. But she's proven her point... she can be up there in the top 10. There are a lotta guys who can't say that."
-- Bobby Unser

Nicknames	Racing Technology	IROC
1 POINT		
1. When he burst onto the NASCAR scene, Dale Earnhardt labeled him simply as "The Kid."	1. If the rear end of the car breaks loose first and the car slides to the wall backwards, what is that called?	1. From 1990 through 1993, the IROC series drivers were racing with what model cars?
2. What track known as 'The Monster Mile' first hosted NASCAR's premier series in 1969?	2. The science of how air flows around a race car is called what?	2. Who is the only driver to win the NASCAR Cup and IROC Championships in the same year?
2 POINTS		
3. Crew chief Mike McSwain is better known in the garage area by what nickname?	3. Can teams test tire compounds on a given race weekend to find the best match for the weather?*	3. In his 15 full IROC seasons, how many times did Dale Earnhardt win the IROC Championship?
4. What top driver earned the nickname 'Rocket Man' since his 2002 rookie season?	4. What is the typical unit of measurement for wedge adjustments?	4. The 2003 IROC season saw what driver score his first IROC series title?
3 POINTS		
5. What former Champion was known as 'The Old Man of the Mountain' before his NASCAR days?	5. What 3 parts of a NASCAR body are supplied by the manufacturer?	5. The first ever IROC Champion was what driver who also won the 1973 NASCAR Cup race in Riverside.**
6. In 1984, Junior Johnson's drivers, Darrell Waltrip and Neil Bonnett, were known collectively as what?	6. A Goodyear Eagle tire ready for NASCAR competition, without the rim, weighs approximately how many pounds?	6. What driver won 2 of 4 races in 2001 to score the IROC Championship?

Contestant	Scoring Area	TALLY

Nicknames	Racing Technology	IROC
1-POINT-ANSWERS		
1. Jeff Gordon	1. Loose (Oversteer)	1. Dodge Daytona
2. Dover International Speedway	2. Aerodynamics	2. Dale Earnhardt - 1990
2-POINT-ANSWERS		
3. 'Fatback'	3. No *	3. 4
4. Ryan Newman	4. Round	4. Kurt Busch
3-POINT-ANSWERS		
5. Rusty Wallace	5. Hood, roof and decklid	5. Mark Donohue**
6. 'Double Bud Thunder'	6. 24	6. Bobby Labonte

* NASCAR and Goodyear cooperate to decide on an optimal
   compound for safety reasons and provide only one rubber
   compound for each race.
** The IROC series that year consisted of 3 road races at Riverside
   and one at Daytona in Porsches. Mark won 3 out of 4 events.

*"Well, there's one thing obvious about the Charger Daytona.
Nobody, but nobody, walks by without breaking his neck to
take a second look."* -- Bobby Isaac's statement to Chrysler
reps after test driving a Dodge Daytona

*"There are always a bunch of stupid moves. Sometimes they
work out and sometimes they don't. Once again, it's
judgmental. A stupid move could be the move that wins
the race."* -- Ryan Newman

All-Star Race	**Jeff Gordon**	**Racing Teams**

1 POINT

1. The All-Star race is primarily for drivers who have done what?

2. Who won the All-Star race in 1992, but crashed just past the finish and went to the hospital instead of victory lane?*

1. In Jeff Gordon's entire NASCAR Cup career, what was the one year he ran but did not win all season?

2. What car owner helped lead Jeff to his first NASCAR Cup title?

1. What car owner holds the record for consecutive NASCAR Cup Championships with 4?

2. Who was the official car owner for Matt Kenseth's championship-winning 2003 NASCAR team?

2 POINTS

3. What year was the very first All-Star race held?

4. What driver debuted a chrome helmet in the 1995 All-Star race that he wore for most of the rest of his career?

3. What NASCAR legend ended his career the same day that Jeff Gordon made his first NASCAR Cup Series start?

4. What year did Jeff win The Winston Million?

3. Who was Dale Earnhardt's first full-time team-mate?**

4. Skipping a race after Davey Allison was killed what driver did Robert Yates hire to drive one race in the #28?

3 POINTS

5. The 2000 All-Star event saw Dale Earnhardt show up in a car painted by what pop artist?

6. The one NASCAR All-Star race that was not in Charlotte was won by what NASCAR legend?

5. At what age did Jeff Gordon start running laps on a track created by his stepfather?

6. Jeff scored his first Busch Series victory at what track?

5. Who took on both car owner and crew chief roles to lead Joe Weatherly to back-to-back Championships?

6. Who was David Pearson's car owner when he won 15 races and the Championship in 1966?

Contestant	Scoring Area	TALLY

All-Star Race	**Jeff Gordon**	**Racing Teams**

1-POINT-ANSWERS

All-Star Race	Jeff Gordon	Racing Teams
1. Won a race in the last year	1. 1993	1. Rick Hendrick
2. Davey Allison*	2. Rick Hendrick	2. Mark Martin

2-POINT-ANSWERS

All-Star Race	Jeff Gordon	Racing Teams
3. 1985	3. Richard Petty	3. Mike Skinner**
4. Darrell Waltrip	4. 1997	4. Robby Gordon

3-POINT-ANSWERS

All-Star Race	Jeff Gordon	Racing Teams
5. Peter Max	5. 5 years old	5. Bud Moore
6. Bill Elliott	6. Atlanta Motor Speedway	6. Cotton Owens

* This race was tagged by Humpy Wheeler as "One Hot Night" and will live forever as one of the great races of all time.
** Mike ran 5 races in 1996 and then ran the full schedule in 1997.

"It's cool to be back. The off-season flew by. I can't believe I'm already in the car. But, things are going well. I felt like they were going to go well based on my talks with Robbie (Loomis) and the team and the work that's been going on with our speedway car and our motors and everything. Over the off-season we felt like we built a car that was a little bit better that the car we had here in July. I felt pretty good about coming into today. So far it's going pretty well and hopefully we can keep that going." -- Jeff Gordon, Jan. 11, 2005, prior to winning the 2005 Daytona 500

TV, Movies & Media	History	Racing Families
1 POINT		
1. Of all of the NASCAR related movies released to date, which one has the highest box office gross?	1. This driver/promoter met with his peers to start an organization that eventually became NASCAR.	1. What famous racing father was in the CBS booth for his son's victory in the 1993 Daytona 500?
2. What nickname does FOX have for their infield pre-race and interview booth?	2. Groundbreaking for what ISC track was done on May 23, 1969?	2. What man was the head of the only four-generation family in NASCAR?
2 POINTS		
3. This NBC personality came over from the MRN radio team to be the play-by-play guy for NBC.	3. The final race of NASCAR's inaugural season took place on what track which, sadly, is no longer on the schedule?	3. In 1998 what family qualified for the entire front row for the Daytona 500?
4. What was the name of the 1977 stock car movie that starred Richard Pryor?	4. What year did ESPN first carry live flag-to-flag NASCAR?	4. In August of 2000, Dale Earnhardt and his 2 sons all started the NASCAR Cup race at what track?
3 POINTS		
5. What cable music channel showed nearly 1/3 of the NASCAR races live from 1991 thru 2000?	5. Although planned, what NASCAR division never got off the ground because it was seen as too "Yankee?"	5. What two family members were running 1-2 when one spun the other during the 1994 Brickyard 400?*
6. What year did CBS pioneer the in-car camera during its broadcast of the Daytona 500?	6. The NASCAR Cup drivers last raced on a dirt track in what year?	6. What little brother of a Busch regular scored his first NASCAR Cup win at Bristol in 2001?

Contestant	Scoring Area	TALLY

TV, Movies & Media	History	Racing Families

1-POINT-ANSWERS

1. 'Days of Thunder'	1. Bill France, Sr.	1. Ned Jarrett
2. 'Hollywood Hotel'	2. Talladega Superspeedway	2. Lee Petty

2-POINT-ANSWERS

3. Allen Bestwick	3. North Wilkesboro	3. Bobby and Terry Labonte
4. 'Greased Lightning'	4. 1981	4. Michigan International Speedway

3-POINT-ANSWERS

5. The Nashville Network (TNN)	5. Roadsters	5. Brett and Geoffrey Bodine*
6. 1979	6. 1970	6. Elliott Sadler

* Brett got into the back of Geoff coming off of turn four.
Brett went on to finish second, Geoffrey was done for the day
and finished 39th.

*"It's hard for me to believe that some of these guys could
pass a driver's test. I can't believe they've got a driver's
license."* -- Mark Martin, after a race at Lowe's Motor Speedway

*"Our piston speeds run up and down the walls faster than
that red little cart that runs around with a Shell sticker on
it."* -- Owner and engine guru Robert Yates, acting as if his
words were possible to understand.

Hendrick Motorsports	Drivers	Great Races
1. Rick Hendrick had his first ten million dollar team when Jeff Gordon cracked that mark in what year?	1. Michael Waltrip's first NASCAR Cup race was in 1985, what year did he score his first Cup series win?	1. Terry Labonte scored his first and last career wins at what race 23 years apart?*
2. The Hendrick Motorsports complex is located very close to what race track?	2. What driver won ten races in a row in 1967?	2. What driver came from 2 laps down at Talladega in 1985 and won the race without catching a caution?

1 POINT

Hendrick Motorsports	Drivers	Great Races
3. At Lowe's Motor Speedway in 1983, what driver brought Hendrick his first Busch series win?	3. In 1993, driving the Robert Yates Racing #28, who scored the first top 5 of his career at Martinsville?	3. Dale Earnhardt holds the record for the fastest 500 miles at Darlington with 139.958 mph, set in what year?
4. Who was the first driver that Rick Hendrick hired to drive for his new team?	4. What driver reached 50 wins the fastest in the history of the sport?	4. The first ever Truck Series race in Darlington was won by what driver in 2001?

2 POINTS

Hendrick Motorsports	Drivers	Great Races
5. When Hendrick rolled into Daytona for his first Daytona 500, what car number was on the door?	5. In 1986, what driver led all NASCAR Cup series drivers with 7 wins on his way to a third place points finish?	5. In 1993, what driver dramatically exited Talladega but was unhurt when rescue crews got to him in the parking lot?
6. The very first sponsor that Hendrick landed was what insurance company?	6. What driver won 4 Most Popular Driver awards in a row from 1980-1983?	6. The last time they raced on the beach in Daytona, who won?

3 POINTS

Contestant	Scoring Area	TALLY

Hendrick Motorsports	Drivers	Great Races
1-POINT-ANSWERS		
1. 2001	1. 2001	1. Southern 500 (1980, 2003)*
2. Lowes Motor Speedway	2. Richard Petty	2. Bill Elliott
2-POINT-ANSWERS		
3. Dale Earnhardt	3. Kenny Wallace	3. 1993
4. Geoff Bodine	4. Jeff Gordon	4. Bobby Hamilton
3-POINT-ANSWERS		
5. 5	5. Tim Richmond	5. Jimmy Horton
6. Northwestern Security Life	6. Bobby Allison	6. Paul Goldsmith

* Editor's Note: Although Labonte is still racing at press time, it is
  assumed that he will not win another race on his limited schedule.

In 1953, Lee Petty drove into the pits of a dirt track race during
a caution period, with his windshield covered in mud. His son
Richard, then a teenager, jumped on the hood and began cleaning it.
The caution car came around and Lee saw that he was about to lose
a lap, so he raced around the track with Richard on the hood and
hanging on for dear life. After making the crucial lap, he pulled
back in to let Richard off. Richard then said...

*"I got the windshield cleaned off. I was afraid if I didn't get
it cleaned off, Daddy'd take me around again."*

*"If you don't have your faith, your family and your friends,
you can't make it through something like this."*
  -- Rick Hendrick, on the plane crash that took the lives of his
  son, brother and key members of his team.

43

Richard Petty	**Craftsman Truck Series**	**Rookies**

1 POINT

1. What driver gave Richard his first win as a car owner after he retired from driving?*

1. What former Truck Series Champion began his career with the Rookie of the Year award in 2001?

1. Of Kurt Busch, Dale Earnhardt Jr., Jimmie Johnson or Ryan Newman which one won the Rookie award?

2. Richard shares the record of 7 championships in a career. What year was his last title?

2. What driver became the first three-time Truck Series champion in 2001?

2. The 2004 NEXTEL Cup Rookie honors went to what Dodge driver?

2 POINTS

3. In 1959, at Lakewood, he thought he had his first win, but what 2nd place driver protested and was given the win?

3. Before 1996, the Craftsman Truck Series vehicles were known by what heroic name?

3. He was the first driver to win the Busch Series title and the Cup Series Rookie honors in the same year.

4. Richard Petty's final NASCAR victory came at what race?

4. What 1997 Truck Series Rookie of the Year also won the 1998 NASCAR Cup rookie honors?

4. What was the most recent year where no rookie won a NASCAR Cup event?

3 POINTS

5. Richard made his NASCAR racing debut in 1958, in the covertible division, at what track?

5. Who was the very first Crafts-man Truck Series Championship car owner?

5. The record for 5 Busch Series wins by a rookie is jointly held by which two drivers?

6. 'King' Richard collected $800 for winning his very first race. The big win came in 1960 at what track?

6. What California race track only saw one Craftsman Truck Series race as Ken Schrader won in 1995?**

6. What driver beat Rusty Wallace for the 1980 Rookie of the Year title?

Contestant	Scoring Area	TALLY

Richard Petty	Craftsman Truck Series	Rookies

1-POINT-ANSWERS

Richard Petty	Craftsman Truck Series	Rookies
1. Bobby Hamilton*	1. Travis Kvapil	1. Ryan Newman
2. 1979	2. Jack Sprague	2. Kasey Kahne

2-POINT-ANSWERS

Richard Petty	Craftsman Truck Series	Rookies
3. Lee Petty - His father	3. SuperTrucks	3. Kevin Harvick
4. Firecracker 400 in Daytona	4. Kenny Irwin Jr.	4. 2004

3-POINT-ANSWERS

Richard Petty	Craftsman Truck Series	Rookies
5. Columbia Speedway (SC)	5. Richard Childress	5. Greg Biffle and Kyle Busch
6. Southern States Fairgrounds in Charlotte	6. Saugus Speedway**	6. Jody Ridley

* The win came in Phoenix International's Dura Lube 500 in 1996.
** This remains as the only race track to be limited to a single truck series race.

"He's a great driver, but he's got some etiquette to learn."
-- Ricky Rudd, referring to Kasey Kahne

"The problem is you've got a young kid who is trying to replace Dale Earnhardt, who thinks he is Dale Earnhardt, and right now he wouldn't be a scab on Dale Earnhardt's butt." -- Bobby Hamilton, on then rookie Kevin Harvick

Racing Rules	**Roush Racing**	**Daytona 500**
1 POINT		
1. If you qualify by the 'Champion's Provisional,' you will take the green flag in what position?	1. After a successful career in other motorsports, Jack Roush started a NASCAR Cup team with what driver?	1. Who was the oldest driver to ever win the Daytona 500?*
2. Lapped cars can move up to the inside on a restart except in the final how many laps?	2. In 2004, Roush Racing had how many full-time NASCAR Cup teams?	2. Name 'The Ultimate Motorsports Attraction' which opened at Daytona Intl. Speedway in 1996?
2 POINTS		
3. The long pieces of aluminum that NASCAR holds against the car to determine if the shape is legal are called what?	3. What driver first won a NASCAR Championship of any type for Jack Roush?	3. In Victory Lane, Darrell Waltrip asked, "This IS the Daytona 500, isn't it?" when he won in what year?
4. The penalty for speeding while leaving your pit stall is what?	4. What year did Jack Roush first go to a multi-car team when he hired Wally Dallenbach as Mark Martin's teammate?	4. Through 2004, who was the last Dodge driver to win the Daytona 500?
3 POINTS		
5. If a driver doesn't lead any laps and finishes 43rd, how many points does he earn?	5. Jack Roush was born on April 19th of what year?	5. Junior Johnson beat more drivers than any other when 68 drivers took the green flag in what year?
6. How many sets of tires are NEXTEL Cup teams allowed to use for practice and qualifying?	6. In October of 1989 Jack Roush's team scored their first NASCAR win at what race track?	6. Who was the first rookie to ever qualify on the front row for the Daytona 500?

Contestant	Scoring Area	TALLY

Racing Rules	Roush Racing	Daytona 500
1-POINT-ANSWERS		
1. 43rd - Last	1. Mark Martin	1. Bobby Allison*
2. 10 laps	2. 5	2. Daytona USA
2-POINT-ANSWERS		
3. Templates	3. Greg Biffle - 1999 Truck series	3. 1989
4. Drive through pits without stopping	4. 1992	4. Ward Burton - 2002
3-POINT-ANSWERS		
5. 34	5. 1942	5. 1960
6. 3 sets	6. North Carolina Motor Speedway	6. Davey Allison - 1987

* Bobby was 50 years, 2 months and 11 days old when he beat his son to the line for the win in 1988.

"Well, my owner (Jack Roush) is crazy." -- Matt Kenseth, after winning the Nextel All-Star Challenge and asked how he won a race usually won 'by drivers who are crazy.'

"I believe we were working on a top-10 (finish) in February and were interrupted by the ever-present flying cars of Daytona." -- Robby Gordon, recalling a crash in the Daytona 500

"The best way to make a small fortune in racing is to start with a big one." -- Junior Johnson

Women In NASCAR	Nicknames	Racing Technology

1 POINT

1. Who was the first lady to ever win a Busch series pole when she took the top spot at Atlanta in 1994?

1. This driver was 'Mr. Excitement,' because exciting things seem to happen near where he is on the track.

1. What is the safety device that fits on the driver's shoulders to hold the head and neck stable in a crash?*

2. What woman is half owner of team that won the 2004 Busch series title?

2. He was known as 'Awesome' before he became 'Million Dollar.'

2. Two cars can go faster than one. On the track this is called what?

2 POINTS

3. Tim Flock once said, "She particularly loved racing with, and beating, her brothers" about what famous NASCAR woman?

3. What former NASCAR Cup Champion has been referred to as 'The Rushville Rocket?'

3. What is the term that describes the amount in inches the two front tires point towards or away from each other?

4. What woman earned $50 in NASCAR's very first event, finishing 14th?

4. New Hampshire International Speedway's official nickname for the oval track is what?

4. The windshield of a NASCAR race car is made of what instead of glass?

3 POINTS

5. What female entered 14 Truck Series events in 2004 scoring a season high 15th in Martinsville?

5. Herb Thomas won it all in 1951 and '53 with a crew chief named Henry. What is Henry better known as?

5. What suspension piece, also called the track bar, attaches the frame to the rear suspension and can be raised or lowered to adjust handling?

6. What woman started her career as a gimmick in 1946 finishing third at Greenville-Pickens?

6. David Pearson dominated Darlington to earn what colorful nickname?

6. NEXTEL Cup cars measure what wheelbase?

Contestant	Scoring Area	TALLY

Women In NASCAR	Nicknames	Racing Technology
1-POINT-ANSWERS		
1. Shawna Robinson	1. Jimmy Spencer	1. HANS Device*
2. Theresa Earnhardt	2. Bill Elliott	2. Drafting
2-POINT-ANSWERS		
3. Ethel Mobley Flock	3. Tony Stewart	3. Toe
4. Sara Christian	4. 'The Magic Mile'	4. Lexan
3-POINT-ANSWERS		
5. Deborah Renshaw	5. 'Smokey Yunick'	5. Panhard bar
6. Louise Smith	6. 'The Silver Fox'	6. 110 Inches

* HANS actually stands for Head And Neck Support. These were mandated in 2001 following the death of Dale Earnhardt.

"I hope my boys make good in racing 'cause they'll starve to death if they don't."
   -- George Elliott (Bill, Ernie and Dave's father)

"All of a sudden, you find yourself and learn that, if you think driving is the only thing you've got to do around here, you're wrong. You've got five or six things to do, and driving is about fifth on the list." -- Jeremy Mayfield

"Anything but first sucks!" -- Dale Earnhardt

Racing Teams	Dale Earnhardt	Champions

1 POINT

Racing Teams

1. How many single-car teams scored NEXTEL Cup wins in 2004?*

2. Darrell Waltrip had what buddy and TV partner as his crew chief for two of his Cup Championships?

Dale Earnhardt

1. What year did Dale Earnhardt Sr. win the NASCAR Rookie of the Year honors?

2. In 2001, Dale Earnhardt teamed with his son to finish fourth in what race?

Champions

1. This driver won the 1995 Winston Cup made of silver (instead of gold) to commemorate Winston's 25th cup with NASCAR.**

2. What driver won the NASCAR Cup Championship in 2000?

2 POINTS

Racing Teams

3. Who was the crew chief for all 3 of Lee Petty's championships?

4. What famous 'gray area' crew chief became a NASCAR official (he was also crew chief for Bobby Allison's 1983 Championship)?

Dale Earnhardt

3. Dale holds the track record for the fastest race ever at what track where he won in 1995 with a 163.633 mph average?

4. What car number did Dale Earnhardt's father drive?

Champions

3. What future Champion won the NASCAR Cup Rookie of the Year title in 1986?

4. In 1990, what driver would have won the Champi-onship if not for a 46 point penalty for an illegal carburetor spacer?

3 POINTS

Racing Teams

5. This car owner made a name in drag racing before Rusty Wallace won him a NASCAR Cham-pionship in 1989.

6. Who was the crew chief on the first NASCAR Championship winning team?

Dale Earnhardt

5. Who was Dale Earnhardt's car owner when he won his first NASCAR Cup?

6. Who was the primary sponsor of Dale Earnhardt's car when he won his first NEXTEL Cup Title?

Champions

5. Joe Weatherly won back-to-back titles in '1962 and '63 for what famous car owner?

6. Matt Kenseth made his Cup series debut in 1998, when he substituted for Bill Elliott at what race track?

Contestant	Scoring Area	TALLY

Racing Teams	Dale Earnhardt	Champions

1-POINT-ANSWERS

Racing Teams	Dale Earnhardt	Champions
1. None*	1. 1979	1. Jeff Gordon**
2. Jeff Hammond	2. Rolex 24 Hours of Daytona	2. Bobby Labonte

2-POINT-ANSWERS

Racing Teams	Dale Earnhardt	Champions
3. Lee Petty	3. Atlanta Motor Speedway	3. Alan Kulwicki
4. Gary Nelson	4. '8'	4. Mark Martin

3-POINT-ANSWERS

Racing Teams	Dale Earnhardt	Champions
5. Raymond Beadle	5. Rod Osterlund	5. Bud Moore
6. Red Vogt	6. Mike Curb Productions	6. Dover Intl. Speedway

* Joe Nemechek in the 01 and his MB2 team are tightly integrated with Scott Riggs' #10 MBV team. No one else is even close to being a single-car operation.

** After losing a close battle, Dale Earnhardt said, with a grin, that he didn't want it anyway because it didn't match the rest of the trophies in his case.

"One of the reasons for my stepping out of the Cup series at this time is because I was never really convinced, deep down inside, that I was all that good. I think I've fooled a lot of people for a long, long time, and I don't want to take a chance on getting caught up in something where everybody figures out that I was a sham and I really wasn't as good as the results I got." -- Mark Martin, announcing his retirement following the 2005 season.

Manufacturers	Race Tracks	History
1 POINT		
1. Chevrolet switched to Monte Carlo in 1995 after racing what model with great success for years?	1. In 1984, what race track saw 75 official lead changes setting a record that still stands today?	1. The 1st meeting of influential racers and promoters that went on to form NASCAR was in what year?*
2. Darrell Waltrip's final NASCAR Cup title came for what car maker?	2. What race track held it's last NEXTEL Cup race in 2004?	2. What year was the final NASCAR race held on the beach in Daytona?
2 POINTS		
3. What make of car was Rusty Wallace driving when he won the 1989 NASCAR Cup title?	3. In 1999, this driver set the record for fastest Michigan race ever at 173.997 mph when he won the caution-free event.	3. One race track from the first NASCAR season - Heidelberg Raceway - was located near what city?
4. Pontiac only won one NASCAR race in 2003, when what driver found Victory Lane in Darlington?	4. What driver swept both Michigan races in 1995?	4. Who won the first NASCAR Cup race on June 19th, 1949?
3 POINTS		
5. In 1966, what manufacturer boycotted in protest over NASCAR rule changes that did not favor them?	5. The records for fastest speed and fewest cautions for 500 laps at Bristol were set by what driver in 1971?**	5. In 1957, all manufacturers pulled out of NASCAR after a crash injured 5 people at this race track.
6. In 1960, what model did Ford return to as their NASCAR Cup race car?	6. The 2003 Craftsman Truck Series visited what track for the first time?	6. How much money did the winner of NASCAR's very first Cup race collect?

Contestant	Scoring Area	TALLY

Manufacturers   Race Tracks   History

1 - P O I N T - A N S W E R S

Manufacturers	Race Tracks	History
1. Lumina	1. Talladega Superspeedway	1. 1947*
2. Chevrolet	2. North Carolina Motor Speedway	2. 1958

2 - P O I N T - A N S W E R S

Manufacturers	Race Tracks	History
3. Pontiac	3. Dale Jarrett	3. Pittsburgh, PA
4. Ricky Craven	4. Bobby Labonte	4. Jim Roper

3 - P O I N T - A N S W E R S

Manufacturers	Race Tracks	History
5. Ford	5. Charlie Glotzbach**	5. Martinsville Speedway
6. Galaxy Starliner	6. Lowes Motor Speedway	6. $2,000

* The meeting was on December 14th of 1947.
** As of February 2005, these records of 101.074 mph and Zero cautions still stand today.

"Tell you what, in the new Charger Daytona, I feel safer at 200 miles per hour than I did at 150 miles per hour in my first race at Daytona in 1961." -- Charlie Glotzbach, June 7, 1970, on his car at Michigan International Speedway

"By the way, I'm not going to give this SuperBee back to the factory. I'm buying it for my wife. She doesn't care if the clutch pedal pressure is a little high. She loves the optional full-synchro 4-speed manual. I told her so." -- Dick Landy, national Super Stock drag racing champion, commenting after a test drive in the 1970 SuperBee

Drivers	**Racing Families**	**Sponsors**
1 POINT		
1. As of February 2005, which driver holds the record for most money earned in one season?*	1. As of 2004, who are the only two siblings to have both won the NASCAR All-Star race?	1. Dale Jarrett beat Dale Earnhardt to the line by .16 sec's to claim the 1993 Daytona 500 for what sponsor?
2. I am second on the all-time win list with 105 career victories. Who am I?	2. What 3 brothers have all won Rookie titles, the oldest in NEXTEL Cup, the younger two in ASA?**	2. Bill Elliott won his Championship with what company as the primary sponsor?
2 POINTS		
3. Who won the Most Popular Driver award more than any other driver during the 1970's?	3. What family-owned NASCAR Cup team made its debut at Martinsville in 1953?	3. What owner/driver scored three NASCAR Cup wins in 1994 driving the Exide Batteries #7?
4. What driver has the most career wins without ever winning a NASCAR Cup Championship?	4. 1960, '65 and '99 saw NASCAR Cup Championships come for what famous racing family?	4. In 1995, Sterling Marlin had three NASCAR Cup wins, including the Daytona 500, for what sponsor?
3 POINTS		
5. In his only full Cup season in 2001, what driver won fans because of his name though he failed to post a top ten finish?	5. Only once have drivers from the same family won the Championship and Rookie honors in the same year... which family?	5. Neil Bonnet's final two victories came in 1988, driving car #75, with what primary sponsor?
6. In 1956, what driver won the first ever most popular driver award?	6. The Bodine family is associated with what New York State hometown?	6. Who was the primary sponsor of NASCAR's very first race winner?

Contestant	Scoring Area	TALLY

Drivers	Racing Families	Sponsors

1-POINT-ANSWERS

Drivers	Racing Families	Sponsors
1. Jeff Gordon*	1. Darrell and Michael Waltrip	1. Interstate Batteries
2. David Pearson	2. Wallace**	2. Coors

2-POINT-ANSWERS

Drivers	Racing Families	Sponsors
3. Richard Petty	3. Wood Brothers Racing	3. Geoffrey Bodine
4. Junior Johnson	4. The Jarretts	4. Kodak

3-POINT-ANSWERS

Drivers	Racing Families	Sponsors
5. Buckshot Jones	5. Lee and Richard Petty - 1959	5. Valvoline
6. Curtis Turner	6. Chemung, NY	6. Mecklenburg Motors

* Winning the Winton No Bull million dollar bonus in Las Vegas and the championship sent Jeff into a new tax bracket as he collected a record $6,649,080 in 2001.

** Rusty Wallace won NASCAR Cup Rookie of the Year in 1984. Kenny did the same for ASA in '86 while Mike won it in '89.

"Race fans, I had inferred from my one trip to the Brickyard 400, fell into one of two categories: tattooed, shirtless, sewer-mouthed drunks, and their husbands." -- Steve Ruchin

"I made as many as four runs a night. I did that from the time I was thirteen until I was in the mid-twenties, 365 days a year, seven or eight times a week, probably more than that." -- Junior Johnson, talking about his bootlegging days

IROC	Busch Series	Jeff Gordon
1 POINT 1. In 2004, the IROC series visited a short track for the first time in series history. Where?	1. What 2003 Busch Championship winning car owner was killed in an airplane crash in 2004?	1. Jeff Gordon is tied for the record for modern-era wins in a single season with what other driver?
2. What driver won an unprecedented three consecutive IROC Championships from 1996-1998?	2. What Mayetta, NJ driver won the 2004 NASCAR Busch Series Championship?	2. What year did Jeff Gordon win the NASCAR Busch series Rookie of the Year award?
2 POINTS 3. What does the acronym, IROC, stand for?	3. What driver went from Rookie of the Year in 1994 to Busch series Champion in 1995, the first to accomplish this feat?	3. In 2000, Jeff Gordon's entire over-the-wall pit crew defected to work for what driver?
4. In 2002, what driver won the IROC title in his first try?	4. Who won the very first Busch series Championship?	4. Jeff Gordon is officially listed as being from what what Indiana hometown?
3 POINTS 5. The 1996 IROC series saw the debut of what sporty race car in the IROC series?	5. From 1982-1984 what driver scored 22 Busch series wins and two Championships to set the standard for everyone who came after?	5. In Jeff's 6 full IROC seasons, how many IROC race wins has he scored?
6. What driver subbed for Alan Kulwicki after his death halfway through the 1993 IROC season?	6. What year was the NASCAR Busch series born?	6. What NEXTEL Cup race typically falls right around Jeff's birthday?

Contestant	Scoring Area	TALLY

IROC	Busch Series	Jeff Gordon

1-POINT-ANSWERS

IROC	Busch Series	Jeff Gordon
1. Richmond International Raceway	1. Ricky Hendrick	1. Richard Petty
2. Mark Martin	2. Martin Truex Jr.	2. 1991

2-POINT-ANSWERS

IROC	Busch Series	Jeff Gordon
3. International Race of Champions	3. Johnny Benson Jr.	3. Dale Jarrett
4. Kevin Harvick	4. Jack Ingram	4. Pittsboro

3-POINT-ANSWERS

IROC	Busch Series	Jeff Gordon
5. Pontiac Firebird Trans-Am	5. Sam Ard	5. One
6. Dale Earnhardt	6. 1982	6. Brickyard 400

"When I was a lap down, I think Jeff (Gordon) was trying to give me a little 'rookie education' when I was behind him. He was waving at me or something. I'm not sure what he was doing. I think he wanted me to back off." -- Casey Atwood

"Don't come here and grumble about going too fast. Get the hell out of the race car if you have feathers on your legs or butt. Put a kerosene rag around your ankles so the ants won't climb up there and eat that candy ass." -- Dale Earnhardt

"The track is so fast, it's not made for racing. It's made for speed." -- Ryan Newman, on Texas Motor Speedway

Richard Petty	Racing Technology	Craftsman Truck Series
1 POINT		
1. In 2000, what company began to phase out their 28 year relationship with Richard Petty?	1. If the front tires lose grip first and the car slides towards the wall, nose first, what is that called?	1. In 2004, what NASCAR sensation entered the first 2 Truck races of his career and won them both?
2. True or False, Richard Petty never earned more than $1,000,000 in a single season as a driver.	2. For 2005, NASCAR limited what to 4 1/2 inches at all non-plate tracks?	2. More common in stick-and-ball sports, the truck series had what until 1998 instead of pit stops?
2 POINTS		
3. Richard Petty won the Rookie title during his first eligible season on the circuit in what year?	3. Nylon webbing, intended to keep the driver's head & arms inside the car in an accident, is called what?	3. What driver won the 1998 Truck Series Rookie of the Year award and then the 2000 Truck Series Championship?
4. Richard won 6 Championships for Chrysler and one for what other manufacturer?*	4. What is the term for the angle at which the tires are tipped in or out?	4. In 2000, who was the first rookie to win back-to-back Truck Series events?
3 POINTS		
5. Richard Petty was born on July 2nd of what year?	5. Name the specific handling problem caused by following another car closely so that less air is hitting the nose?	5. Who won the first Craftsman Truck Series race ever?
6. In 1965, NASCAR declared his engine illegal, Chrysler boycotted NASCAR, and Richard did what during most of the 1965 season?	6. Nomex is a brand name owned by what popular NASCAR company?	6. What Truck Series track is the only Cup, Busch or Truck track that also hosts weekly short track racing?

Contestant	Scoring Area	TALLY

Richard Petty	Racing Technology	Craftsman Truck Series

1-POINT-ANSWERS

Richard Petty	Racing Technology	Craftsman Truck Series
1. STP	1. Push (Understeer)	1. Kasey Kahne
2. True - Richard's best year was $508,884 in 1983	2. Rear spoiler	2. Halftime Break

2-POINT-ANSWERS

Richard Petty	Racing Technology	Craftsman Truck Series
3. 1959	3. Window Net	3. Greg Biffle
4. Chevrolet*	4. Camber	4. Kurt Busch

3-POINT-ANSWERS

Richard Petty	Racing Technology	Craftsman Truck Series
5. 1937	5. Aero Push	5. Mike Skinner
6. Drag Racing	6. DuPont	6. Mansfield Motorsports Park (OH)

* NASCAR declared the Dodge Charger body illegal after the 1977 season and Chrysler's replacement Dodge Magnum wasn't up to speed so Richard Petty switched to Chevy for the 1979 season and won his seventh title.

Funny Quotes by Murray Walker

"The lead car is absolutely unique, except for the one behind it which is identical"

"Alain Prost is in a commanding second position."

"There are four different cars filling the first four places."

"The lead is now 6.9 seconds. In fact it's just under 7 seconds."

Brickyard 400	Great Races	Coca-Cola 600

1 POINT

1. In 2002, Dodge won its only Brickyard 400 to date. What driver took the win that day?

2. The first ever Brickyard 400 was held at Indianapolis Motor Speedway in 1994, who won?

1. After tragedy struck Daytona in February, 2001, he won the emotional Pepsi 400 in July that year.

2. What driver won the final Southern 500 when he took the race in November, 2004?

1. Dubbed 'The Greatest Showman on Earth,' who is the president and promoter at Lowes Motor Speedway?

2. What driver won the Coca-Cola 600 during his 2000 rookie season?

2 POINTS

3. The great Dale Earnhardt Sr. won one Brickyard 400 in his career. What year did he get his win?

4. Who started on the pole for the first Brickyard 400 (1994)?

3. In 1992 concrete replaced the old asphalt in Bristol. Who won the first race on the new surface?

4. New Hampshire once had a single driver lead every lap of the Cup race. Who won that day?*

3. What year did the Coca-Cola 600 first race under the lights with its current day-into-night format?

4. Who was the first driver to compete in the Indy 500 and the Coca-Cola 600 on the same day?

3 POINTS

5. The slowest Brickyard, when it had 13 cautions totalling more that 1/4 of the race, was what year?

6. Who was the only non-American to start any of the first ten Brickyard 400 races?

5. What driver, with a great name for racing, scored his only NASCAR Cup series win at Darlington in 1988?

6. In 1980, what NASCAR driver won the final Cup race at Ontario Motor Speedway?

5. Mercury found Victory Lane at the Coca-Cola 600 for the last time in 1976, when what driver won his final 600?

6. Who was the last Dodge driver to win the 600?

Contestant	Scoring Area	TALLY

Brickyard 400	**Great Races**	**Coca-Cola 600**

1-POINT-ANSWERS

Brickyard 400	Great Races	Coca-Cola 600
1. Bill Elliott	1. Dale Earnhardt, Jr.	1. HA "Humpy" Wheeler
2. Jeff Gordon	2. Jimmie Johnson	2. Matt Kenseth

2-POINT-ANSWERS

Brickyard 400	Great Races	Coca-Cola 600
3. 1995	3. Darrell Waltrip	3. 1993
4. Rick Mast	4. Jeff Burton*	4. John Andretti

3-POINT-ANSWERS

Brickyard 400	Great Races	Coca-Cola 600
5. 2004 - 115.037 mph	5. Lake Speed	5. David Pearson
6. Geoff Brabham (Australia) Raced in 1994	6. Benny Parsons	6. Richard Petty - 1977

* This race was September of 2000, when restrictor plates were used at the speedway for safety reasons.

"The only way he was gonna beat us was if we wrecked - so he came up there and took us out himself."
   -- Matt Kenseth on Dale Earnhardt, Jr

"I don't have near as much common sense as he had, and he banked on that just about all day, every day, of his life."
   -- Dale Earnhardt Jr., comparing himself to his father

"Do you think you'll be driving a race car for the rest of your life?"-- Matt Kenseth's high school English teacher

"You win some, lose some, and wreck some."
   -- Dale Earnhardt

	Race Tracks	**Women In NASCAR**	**Nicknames**
1 POINT	1. What famous race course ranged from 4.10 to 4.17 miles on mixed surfaces through its history?	1. She became the first woman to compete in a Truck Series event when she started at Walt Disney World Speedway in 1997.	1. What driver's qualifying prowess earned him the nickname 'Front Row?'
	2. What driver is the all-time leader in poles at Darlington?	2. In 1986 who became the first woman to lead a Busch Series event?	2. North Carolina Speedway is best known by what nickname, that might better suited for a professional wrestler?
2 POINTS	3. What Busch and Truck series short track is .686 miles with 12 degrees of progressive banking in the turns?	3. What famous female started 19 Cup races in 1977, scoring four top tens in the Kelly Girl Chevy?	3. When a caution flag flies, the rules allow for the first driver with one lap down to get his lap back for free. What is this rule called?
	4. The Aarons 499 at Talladega is how many laps long?	4. What female driver made her NEXTEL Cup debut at Michigan in 2001?	4. Which race track has been called 'The Diamond in the Desert?'
3 POINTS	5. What 17 year old future country music legend sang the National Anthem for the first race at Bristol in 1961?	5. Who began her NASCAR career with a lap two crash in the 2004 Busch series race in Homestead?	5. Cale Yarborough branded this young driver 'Jaws' because of his brash character.
	6. From 1963 to 1965, Fred Lorenzen won four in-a-row at what short track?	6. What woman raced in two events in 1949, with a best finish of 11th on the beach at Daytona?	6. 'Lone Star JR' has one NASCAR points win to his credit. What is this famous driver's real name?*

Contestant	Scoring Area	TALLY

Women In NASCAR

Race Tracks	Women In NASCAR	Nicknames

1-POINT-ANSWERS

Race Tracks	Women In NASCAR	Nicknames
1. Daytona Beach / Road Course	1. Tammy Jo Kirk	1. Joe Nemechek
2. David Pearson	2. Patty Moise	2. 'The Rock'

2-POINT-ANSWERS

Race Tracks	Women In NASCAR	Nicknames
3. Indianapolis Raceway Park	3. Janet Guthrie	3. 'Lucky Dog'
4. 188	4. Shawna Robinson	4. Las Vegas Motor Speedway

3-POINT-ANSWERS

Race Tracks	Women In NASCAR	Nicknames
5. Brenda Lee	5. Jennifer Cobb	5. Darrell Waltrip
6. Martinsville Speedway	6. Ethel Mobley Flock	6. Johnny Rutherford*

* Johnny Rutherford won a Daytona qualifying race in 1963. Back then the qualifiers counted for points so this is credited as an official race win.

"One of the best races of the afternoon was between Bobby Allison and Janet Guthrie. They swapped positions back and forth and ran side by side trying to outbrave each other in action that had the veterans shaking their heads. It was some fine show."-- Stock Car Racing Magazine, on the race at Ontario, CA, Nov. 20, 1977

"Darrell (Waltrip) was a finesse driver, but he would trick you to death. He would hold back so much, he would almost lose the race. I would say, 'Hey Cale, are you laying down on me?' He would say, 'Junior, my name is Darrell, it ain't Cale.'" -- Junior Johnson

All-Star Race	Daytona 500	Busch Series

1 POINT

1. What driver started the 'special paint scheme' era when he drove a silver car in the 1995 All-Star race?*

1. The first Daytona 500 was held on the high-banked 2 1/2 mile speedway on February 22nd of what year?

1. What driver won the 2003 NASCAR Busch Series Championship?

2. Jeff Gordon won his first All-Star race and first Championship in what year?

2. Which car maker has won more Daytona 500s than any other?

2. What future star scored five Busch wins en route to the 2004 Busch series 'Rookie of the Year' honors?

2 POINTS

3. Qualifying for the All-Star race is unique because it is the only qualifying event that requires what?

3. What driver holds the record for the most consecutive Daytona 500 starts with 32?

3. Rookie of the Year was first awarded in the Busch series in 1989 when what driver received the honor?

4. Who is the only driver in All-Star race history to win back-to-back events?

4. What is the name of the trophy that the winner of the Daytona 500 receives?

4. What Pontiac driver won the very first Busch series race?

3 POINTS

5. Darrell Waltrip was only a lap from the checkers in 1989 when he got punted for the win by what driver?

5. Lee Petty was declared the winner of the 1959 Daytona 500, three days after what driver celebrated in Victory Lane?**

5. What driver won 8 of the 11 Busch races held at North Carolina Motor Speedway from Oct., 1992 through Oct., 1997?

6. In 1992, the All-Star race featured what for the very first time?

6. What racing legend scored his only NASCAR victory at the 1967 Daytona 500?

6. What owner won three Busch series titles in a row with two different drivers?†

Contestant	Scoring Area	TALLY

All-Star Race	Daytona 500	Busch Series

1-POINT-ANSWERS

All-Star Race	Daytona 500	Busch Series
1. Dale Earnhardt*	1. 1959	1. Brian Vickers
2. 1995	2. Chevrolet	2. Kyle Busch

2-POINT-ANSWERS

All-Star Race	Daytona 500	Busch Series
3. A pit stop	3. Dave Marcis	3. Kenny Wallace
4. Davey Allison	4. Harley J. Earl Trophy	4. Dale Earnhardt

3-POINT-ANSWERS

All-Star Race	Daytona 500	Busch Series
5. Rusty Wallace	5. Johnny Beauchamp**	5. Mark Martin
6. It was run under the lights	6. Mario Andretti	6. Bill Baumgardner †

* This was in honor of RJ Reynolds' 25th anniversary in NASCAR.
** This was a three-wide photo finish with the lapped car of Joe Weatherly on the outside. Newsreel footage determined the winner on Wednesday after the race was long over.
† Bill was Johnny Benson's car owner in 1994 and again when Randy Lajoie won the title in 95 and 96.

"We've always raced each other hard. As everybody knows, Earnhardt's a tough competitor. Even when we're racing go-karts at the NASCAR SpeedPark, he's a tough guy to beat."-- Dale Jarrett on Dale Earnhardt

"I looked over and I said, 'What the hell are you doing on the apron, again?' He's got something for those aprons.'"
-- Rusty Wallace (spun after contacting Jeff Gordon at Louden)

Dale Earnhardt	**Rookies**	**Racing History**
1 POINT		
1. What year did Dale Earnhardt make his first NASCAR Cup start?	1. To warn other drivers, what color tape is required on the back bumper of all rookie cars?	1. Before Bill France showed up, what type of motorsports was already running on Daytona beach?
2. Where did Dale Earnhardt score his final NASCAR Cup win?	2. What year did Dale Earnhardt win the NASCAR Cup Rookie title?	2. What is the claim to fame of Daytona Beach's Streamline Inn Motel?
2 POINTS		
3. What car number was Dale driving when he won his first NASCAR Championship?	3. Who was the last driver to win a race and still be eligible for the next season's 'Rookie of the Year' award?*	3. All but one of the races on the original NASCAR schedule were scheduled for how many laps?
4. What feat did Dale Earnhardt Jr. accomplish twice (in 1998 and 1999) that his father never did?	4. Only one rookie won a race during the 2003 NEXTEL Cup season. Who was that?	4. How many races made up the first NASCAR Championship season?
3 POINTS		
5. Dale Earnhardt scored his first career pole at a road course in his rookie year. What year did he score his only road win?	5. What road race ace won the 1973 Rookie honors and credits among his wins the 2002 Sonoma race?	5. NASCAR's first race on a fully paved race track came in June of 1950 at what race track?
6. What year did Dale Earnhardt win the final Busch race of his career?**	6. Mark Martin finished second in the 'Rookie of the Year' standings to what other driver?	6. Erwin "Cannonball" Baker took on what role when NASCAR was first formed?

Contestant	Scoring Area	TALLY

Dale Earnhardt	Rookies	Racing History
1-POINT-ANSWERS		
1. 1975	1. Yellow	1. Land Speed Record Attempts
2. Talladega - Oct. 15, 2000	2. 1979	2. It was the site of the first meeting of NASCAR
2-POINT-ANSWERS		
3. # 2	3. Jamie McMurray*	3. 200
4. Win the Busch Series Championship	4. Greg Biffle	4. 8
3-POINT-ANSWERS		
5. 1995 (Sears Point)	5. Ricky Rudd	5. Dayton, OH
6. 1994**	6. Geoffrey Bodine	6. Commissioner of Racing

* Jamie won in Charlotte in 2002 in only his second start and went on to win the Rookie of the Year honors in 2003.
** Earnhardt won in February in Daytona. 1994 was also the last year that Earnhardt raced in the Busch series.

"Don't come here and grumble about going too fast. Get out of the racecar if you've got feathers on your legs or butt. Put a kerosene-soaked rag around your ankles so the ants won't climb up there and eat your candy a**."
-- Dale Earnhardt, on slowing down races

Drivers	Technology	Richard Petty

1 POINT

1. What 'wing-tipped' driver scored the first win of his long career at Martinsville Speedway in '75?

1. Since 2002, NASCAR has required what high-tech gadget better known for collecting airplane crash data?

1. Richard's richest single victory of his career was $90,575, in 1981, when he won what prestigious race?

2. What driver holds the record for the most wins in a single season?

2. At all non-restrictor plate tracks, what is the maximum capacity of the fuel tank?

2. Who sang the Rodney Crowell-written 'Oh, King Richard' on 1995's NASCAR Runnin' Wide Open album?

2 POINTS

3. Now a car owner, who only managed a best finish of third in 285 career starts as a driver?

3. As racers transitioned from street cars to true race cars, what safety innovation became mandatory in 1952?

3. In 1969 Richard shocked Mopar fans when he left Plymouth for what manufacturer?

4. What driver posted a stunning 5.7 average finish with a full 33 starts in 1998?

4. What is the maximum displacement in cubic inches of a NEXTEL Cup engine?

4. What year did Richard Petty first race with the familiar red and blue STP paint scheme?

3 POINTS

5. What legendary driver scored the first two NASCAR wins of his career in the 1964 and 1965 Firecracker 400s?

5. Tim Flock was disqualified from winning the 1952 Daytona Beach race because what was found to be wooden?

5. After entering NASCAR in 1958, what year did Richard first compete in every single Cup event on the schedule?**

6. What driver holds the record for the fastest NASCAR Cup race ever?*

6. What company built the first purpose-built racing tire in 1952?

6. In six IROC seasons, how many total wins did Richard score in the series?

Contestant	Scoring Area	TALLY

Drivers	**Technology**	**Richard Petty**

1-POINT-ANSWERS

Drivers	Technology	Richard Petty
1. Dave Marcis	1. Black box	1. Daytona 500
2. Richard Petty - 27 in 1967	2. 22 gallons	2. Kyle Petty

2-POINT-ANSWERS

Drivers	Technology	Richard Petty
3. Richard Childress	3. Roll Cages	3. Ford
4. Jeff Gordon	4. 358ci	4. 1972

3-POINT-ANSWERS

Drivers	Technology	Richard Petty
5. AJ Foyt	5. His roll-cage	5. 1968**
6. Mark Martin*	6. Pure Oil Company	6. Zero

* Mark won Talladega in October of 1997 when the race went
   caution free. His average speed was 188.354 MPH.

** In the early days of NASCAR it wasn't unusual for drivers to not
   travel to every event. Richard won 2 Championships before he
   ever completed a full schedule.

*"Why did I take up racing? I was too lazy to work and too
   chicken to steal."* --Kyle Petty

*"I don't think our system of provisional starting spots is
   right. The nature of this sport is competition; to me, you're
   either fast enough or you don't make the show. Do the
   Green Bay Packers get a free spot in the playoffs just
   because they won some Super Bowls?"* -- Dave Marcis

*"Racing cars is not the safest thing. Maybe at times it's
   not the sanest thing."* -- Michael Waltrip

TV, Movies & Media	IROC	Racing Families
1 POINT		
1. Before flag-to-flag coverage, Americans used to occasionally see the start, finish and all the wrecks on what ABC show?	1. Three drivers have won an IROC Championship without winning a NASCAR race and they all share what last name? *	1. What former driver cheered his little brother to victory in the Daytona 500 as a Fox television commentator?
2. Tom Cruise's character was named what in 'Days of Thunder'?	2. In 2004, what driver claimed $1 million for winning the IROC Championship?	2. Which Burton brother was the first to win a NASCAR Cup race?
2 POINTS		
3. "NASCAR 3D" was narrated by what Hollywood star?	3. 1997 saw what driver become the first Busch series regular to win an IROC race?	3. What brothers both drove for Diamond Ridge Motorsports in the 1998 Busch series campaign?
4. In 1983, Burt Reynolds starred in this movie about the perils of an overzealous NASCAR sponsor.	4. What two drivers share the record for career IROC Series Championships?	4. Through 2004, what family-owned NASCAR team had a total of 97 Cup victories?
3 POINTS		
5. Who was the anchor in the broadcast booth for the first network broadcast of the Daytona 500?**	5. What 2-time IROC champion never finished lower than 2nd in the standings in his first five IROC seasons?	5. What driver made his Cup debut at Nashville Raceway in 1976 after his father broke his shoulder and could not race?
6. MRN's first live NASCAR broadcast was the Daytona 500 in what year?	6. Who was the first driver to win back-to-back IROC Championships?	6. In 2000, what brothers became the first to have both won Busch titles?†

Contestant	Scoring Area	TALLY

TV, Movies & Media	IROC	Racing Families

1-POINT-ANSWERS

1. Wide World of Sports	1. Unser*	1. Darrell Waltrip for Michael
2. Cole Trickle	2. Matt Kenseth	2. Ward - 1995 - Rockingham

2-POINT-ANSWERS

3. Kiefer Sutherland	3. Randy Lajoie	3. The Sadlers
4. 'Stroker Ace'	4. Mark Martin & Dale Earnhardt	4. Wood Brothers Racing

3-POINT-ANSWERS

5. Ken Squire**	5. Al Unser Jr.	5. Sterling Marlin
6. 1970	6. AJ Foyt	6. David and Jeff Green†

* Bobby won in 1975, Al Sr. in 1978 and Little Al in 1986 and again in 1988.

** The only other guy on the booth that day was British driver David Hobbes while Ned Jarrett and Brock Yates worked pit road.

† Jeff Green won the Busch series championship in 2000 while older brother David won his title in 1994.

"My dad's pretty special. I still remember the day he told my mother I was gonna race at NASCAR's fastest speedway. Daddy was spearing a piece of meat at dinner. Looking away from her he said, 'Pass the potatoes Eula Faye. Sterling's running at Talladega this weekend.'"
-- Sterling Marlin

Champions	Racing Teams	Race Tracks
1 POINT		
1. Robbie Loomis was the crew chief for what 2001 NASCAR Championship driver?	1. Who was the crew chief for Tony Stewart's NEXTEL Cup Championship?	1. What NASCAR Cup track is 2 1/2 miles long, but only has 9 degrees of banking in the turns?
2. What driver scored Championships for both Billy Hagan and Rick Hendrick?	2. Robert Yates Racing won their first NASCAR Cup victory with what driver behind the wheel?	2. What track boasts the longest straightaway in all of NASCAR?*
2 POINTS		
3. Who is the only driver to win three consecutive NASCAR Cup Championships?	3. What driver gave Richard Childress his first win as a NASCAR Cup car owner?	3. From 1970 through 1981 the first race of the NASCAR Cup season was held at what race track?
4. Matt Kenseth only won one race during his Championship season in 2003. What race track did he conquer?	4. With 10 wins, what car owner scored the most NASCAR Cup victories in 1993?**	4. In 1998, the Busch Series started racing at what Colorado track?
3 POINTS		
5. Winning the title in 1951 and again in 1953, who became the first 2-time Champion?	5. In 1986, the Stavola Bros. saw each of their drivers win a race for Miller Beer. Bobby Allison and who else?	5. Phoenix International saw this driver win 3 Craftsman Truck Series races in a row from 1996-97.
6. What driver won only one race in his NASCAR career, but also managed to win a Championship?	6. What driver brought the Wood Brothers their first NASCAR Cup victory?	6. What legendary N.Carolina 1/4 mile track hosted NASCAR Cup racing from 1958 through 1971?

Contestant	Scoring Area	TALLY

Champions	Racing Teams	Race Tracks

1-POINT-ANSWERS

Champions	Racing Teams	Race Tracks
1. Jeff Gordon	1. Greg Zipadelli	1. Indianapolis Motor Speedway
2. Terry Labonte	2. Davey Allison	2. Talladega Superspeedway*

2-POINT-ANSWERS

Champions	Racing Teams	Race Tracks
3. Cale Yarborough	3. Ricky Rudd	3. Riverside International Raceway
4. Las Vegas Motor Speedway	4. Roger Penske**	4. Pikes Peak International Raceway

3-POINT-ANSWERS

Champions	Racing Teams	Race Tracks
5. Herb Thomas	5. Bobby Hillin Jr.	5. Jack Sprague
6. Bill Rexford	6. Speedy Thompson	6. Bowman-Gray Stadium

* The back straightaway at Talladega measures a massive 4,000 ft.
** All ten of these wins were with Rusty Wallace who went on to finish 2nd in points behind Dale Earnhardt.

"Most of them drivers I had in their prime, and that makes a difference. Cale (Yarborough) wrecked the first eight races he drove for us. My boys said, 'What are you going to do with that crazy fool? He's going to wreck every car we've got.' I said, 'He's going to learn every time you hit that wall, it hurts worse and worse.' As he wrecked those cars, he became one of the best drivers I had." -- Junior Johnson

Jeff Gordon	Craftsman Truck Series	Racing Rules
1 POINT 1. What race track saw Jeff Gordon score his very first NASCAR Cup points-paying race?	1. What former NASCAR Cup racer claimed his first Craftsman Truck Series title as both owner and driver in 2004?	1. What signal can a driver who was involved in a crash give to indicate to safety workers that he is okay?
2. What year did Jeff Gordon make his first NASCAR NEXTEL Cup series start?	2. What driver was the first ever NASCAR Craftsman Truck Series Champion?	2. As of 2004, a driver who wins and leads the most laps earns how many points?
2 POINTS 3. Where did Jeff Gordon first meet his future (and now former) wife Brooke Sealy?*	3. What track hosted the first official NASCAR Craftsman Truck Series race?	3. After receiving a black flag, how long does a driver have before he must obey it?
4. Jeff is tied for the record for modern era wins in a single season with how many?	4. In 2000, what future NASCAR Cup star was the Truck Series 'Rookie of the Year'?	4. Under caution, if you enter the pits before they are officially open what is the penalty?
3 POINTS 5. Jeff Gordon became the first driver to ever win the Winston 'No Bull' bonus when he collected a big win at what race track in 1998?	5. 2002 and 2003 saw what truck owner win back-to-back Truck Series titles with 2 different drivers?	5. The area where NASCAR inspection takes place has what intimidating nickname?
6. Jeff was born on August 4th of what year?	6. The truck series 100th race was at Evergreen Speedway in 1999. Who won this historic race?	6. What driver won the race the first time that the NEXTEL Cup green/white/ checkers rule was put into effect?**

Contestant	Scoring Area	TALLY

Jeff Gordon / Craftsman Truck Series / Racing Rules

Jeff Gordon	Craftsman Truck Series	Racing Rules

1-POINT-ANSWERS

Jeff Gordon	Craftsman Truck Series	Racing Rules
1. Lowes Motor Speedway	1. Bobby Hamilton	1. Put the window net down
2. 1992	2. Mike Skinner	2. 190

2-POINT-ANSWERS

Jeff Gordon	Craftsman Truck Series	Racing Rules
3. Victory Lane at Daytona*	3. Phoenix International Raceway	3. 5 laps
4. 13	4. Kurt Busch	4. Restart at the end of the longest line

3-POINT-ANSWERS

Jeff Gordon	Craftsman Truck Series	Racing Rules
5. Indianapolis Motor Speedway	5. Steve Coulter	5. 'The Room of Doom'
6. 1971	6. Ron Hornaday Jr.	6. Jeff Gordon**

* Jeff had just won a Gatorade Twin 125 qualifying race for the 1993 Daytona 500. Brooke was in Victory Lane getting her picture taken with Jeff because she was Miss Winston at the time.
** The green/white/checkers rule was implemented in NEXTEL Cup racing for the first time on August 8th 2004 during the Brickyard 400.

"Around the track, Brooke (Gordon) isn't looked upon as a beauty queen anymore; she's portrayed as the ice princess. The former Miss Winston is now about as welcome around here as a nicotine patch. When her name is mentioned, these good ol' boys scrunch up their noses as if you offered them a six-pack of O'Doul's."

-- Mike Bianchi, Orlando Sentinel Reporter

Race Tracks	Sponsors	Manufacturers
1 POINT		
1. Since 1969, Bristol Motor Speedway has featured how many degrees of banking in the turns?	1. The Hooters car won the 1992 NASCAR Cup title with what driver behind the wheel?	1. In 2005, Dodge switched its car over to the legendary Charger. What model did it use before that?
2. What is the longest race track on the NASCAR NEXTEL Cup circuit?	2. NASCAR's first title series sponsor was what brand that became synonymous with the sport?	2. What driver gave Pontiac its last NASCAR NEXTEL Cup Championship?
2 POINTS		
3. What New York State track hosted NASCAR Cup racing in 1970 and '71, with Richard Petty taking both races?	3. Tim Richmond, Mark Martin and Ken Schrader all won NASCAR Cup races for what primary sponsor?	3. What car maker boycotted NASCAR in 1965 when its racing engine was declared illegal for competition?
4. Before 1989 Talladega Superspeedway was known by what name?	4. What sponsor did Darrell Waltrip carry to his only Daytona 500 victory?	4. Jeff Gordon claimed his first Busch Series race for what manufacturer?
3 POINTS		
5. In 1951, 1969 and 1970, what Connecticut track hosted the only NASCAR Cup racing in state history?	5. Bobby Labonte won the 1991 Busch Series Championship with what primary sponsor?	5. What defunct car maker won 3 consecutive manufacturers titles from 1952 to 1954?
6. In 1991-'92, what driver became the first back-to-back winner in Phoenix?	6. Harry Gant has 18 career NASCAR Cup victories, all with what primary sponsor?	6. What manufacturer won the final race on the old Beach course in Daytona?

Contestant	Scoring Area	TALLY

Race Tracks	**Sponsors**	**Manufacturers**

1-POINT-ANSWERS

Race Tracks	Sponsors	Manufacturers
1. 36 degrees	1. Alan Kulwicki	1. Intrepid R/T
2. Talladega	2. Winston	2. Tony Stewart

2-POINT-ANSWERS

Race Tracks	Sponsors	Manufacturers
3. Albany-Saratoga Speedway	3. Folgers Coffee	3. Chrysler
4. Alabama International Motor Speedway	4. Tide	4. Ford

3-POINT-ANSWERS

Race Tracks	Sponsors	Manufacturers
5. Thompson Speedway	5. Penrose Pickled Sausage	5. Hudson
6. Davey Allison	6. Skoal Bandit	6. Pontiac

"It's basically the same, just darker." -- Alan Kulwicki, on racing Saturday nights as opposed to Sunday afternoons

"When today's race is over, it's over. The only race that matters is the one coming up." -- Harry Gant

"NASCAR has proven time and time again that they're willing to change the rules at any time for any or no reason. I don't get too excited about rules anymore because they could change at any time." -- Tony Stewart

"I guess he lives up to that commercial where he plays the Tasmanian Devil. His wild side comes out." -- Bobby Labonte, on Dale Earnhardt

Great Races	Brickyard 400	Daytona 500

1 POINT

1. Dale Earnhardt punted Terry Labonte out of the way to win under the lights at Bristol in what year?

2. In 1989, Ricky Rudd won the first Cup race held at what unique race track?

1. Who was the first non-Chevy driver to win the Brickyard 400?

2. What driver holds the record for the most Brickyard 400 victories?

1. Who holds the record for the most Daytona 500 victories?

2. Who won the 1976 Daytona 500, surviving a last lap wreck to creep over the finish line on the apron?*

2 POINTS

3. In 2004, Matt Kenseth and Kevin Harvick were fined and penalized for incidents at what track?

4. Jeff Gordon captured The Winston Million in 1997 by winning at which three race tracks?

3. What year did the Brickyard 400 feature a record-setting 21 lead changes?

4. Who is the only driver to win from the pole in the first 10 years of the Brickyard 400?

3. What driver won the 1988 Daytona 500 which was very first restrictor plate race ever?

4. What motor - sports superstar brought the Wood Brothers a victory in the 1972 Daytona 500?

3 POINTS

5. Trenton Speed-way featured a unique kidney shape when Bobby Allison was the track's last winner in what year?

6. Who won the inaugural NASCAR Cup series race held at Las Vegas Motor Speedway?

5. After starting on the pole in 1997 and 1998; 2nd in 1996 would be this driver's best career Brickyard finish?

6. With NASCAR in its future, what year was the Indianapolis Motor Speedway built?

5. The winner of the Daytona 500 received more than $1,000,000 for the first time in what year?

6. What driver set a record for leading the most laps without winning when he lead 170 laps in 1961?

Contestant	Scoring Area	TALLY

Great Races	**Brickyard 400**	**Daytona 500**

1-POINT-ANSWERS

Great Races	Brickyard 400	Daytona 500
1. 1999	1. Dale Jarrett - 1996	1. Richard Petty with 7
2. Infineon Raceway	2. Jeff Gordon	2. David Pearson*

2-POINT-ANSWERS

Great Races	Brickyard 400	Daytona 500
3. Pocono	3. 1994	3. Bobby Allison
4. Daytona, Charlotte and Darlington	4. Kevin Harvick	4. AJ Foyt

3-POINT-ANSWERS

Great Races	Brickyard 400	Daytona 500
5. 1972	5. Ernie Irvan	5. 1998
6. Mark Martin	6. 1909	6. Fireball Roberts

* Pearson passed Richard Petty on the final lap, then Petty was passing him back when the two crashed just short of the finish line. Petty was done but Pearson was able to creep over the line for the win.

"Didn't mean to spin him out, I just meant to rattle his cage." -- Dale Earnhardt regarding the Terry Labonte spin

"I guess a lot of fans were eating a lot of stuff. We'd prefer that they throw their wrappers in a trash bag next time." -- Dale Jarrett, after a California race was stopped for workers to pick up trash thrown on the track

"I'm not quite ready to kick a** and take names, but I am taking names." -- William C. France, while recovering from illness at Daytona

History	Busch Series	Rookies
1 POINT		
1. Darlington Raceway would have been a true oval but the original design was altered to avoid what?	1. In 1998 and again in 1999, what driver won back-to-back Busch series Chamionships?	1. What driver won a Gatorade 125 mile qualifier in his very first attempt as a rookie driver in 1993?
2. What was the longest race track on the inaugural NASCAR Cup schedule?	2. In 2002, what driver brought Jack Roush his first Busch Series Championship?	2. 2004 saw what young driver win the Busch series 'Rookie if the Year' title?
2 POINTS		
3. Who won the opening race at Talladega Superspeedway for the only victory of his career?	3. What Busch Series owner/driver won his very first start as a car owner in Richmond of 2002?	3. After winning Rookie of the Race at the 1980 Indy 500 what driver began his full-time NASCAR Cup career in 1981?
4. Construction of Daytona International Speedway began in what year?	4. What current NASCAR Cup star scored the Busch series Championship in 1991?	4. Who was the 2003 NASCAR Cup 'Rookie of the Year'?
3 POINTS		
5. What company did Bill France Sr. work for when motor racing halted during World War II?	5. What current Cup driver won the 1992 Busch series Championship as both driver and car owner?**	5. What driver won the NASCAR Cup Rookie title in 1990 despite being killed in an off-track auto accident in September?
6. The first NASCAR race at Bristol Motor Speedway was held on July 30, 1961. Who won?*	6. What NASCAR legend was Larry Pearson's car owner for his Busch series titles in 1986 and 1987?	6. What year did Kenny Schrader win 'Rookie of the Year' honors?

Contestant	Scoring Area	TALLY

History	**Busch Series**	**Rookies**

1-POINT-ANSWERS

History	Busch Series	Rookies
1. Mr. Ramsey's Minnow Pond	1. Dale Earnhardt Jr.	1. Jeff Gordon
2. Daytona Beach / Road Course	2. Greg Biffle	2. Kyle Busch

2-POINT-ANSWERS

History	Busch Series	Rookies
3. Richard Brickhouse	3. Dale Earnhardt Jr.	3. Tim Richmond
4. 1957	4. Bobby Labonte	4. Jamie McMurray

3-POINT-ANSWERS

History	Busch Series	Rookies
5. Daytona Boat Works	5. Joe Nemechek**	5. Rob Moroso
6. Jack Smith*	6. David Pearson	6. 1985

* Jack only drove the first 290 laps Johnny Allen relieved him and was behind the wheel at the checkers. The two split the prize money, taking home $1,612.50 each.

** Joe also won the Most Popular Driver award for the Busch Series that same year

---

"Everybody else got by us, but that cue-bald-headed fool can't get by us without wrecking us." -- Dale Earnhardt, Jr. referring to the follicle-challenged Todd Bodine

"All of the drivers here I can speak to because they all speak English, with the exception of Ward Burton. He speaks Ward, I guess." -- Tony Stewart on the difference between NASCAR and IRL

Hendrick Motorsports	Nicknames	TV, Movies & Media

1 POINT

1. In 1986, Rick Hendrick first went to a two car team when he hired who as his second driver?

1. 'The Bowtie Brigade' is often used to describe all drivers who use cars by what manufacturer?

1. Lindsay Lohan stars in the 2005 movie where what famous, funny race car takes on NASCAR?

2. What driver brought Rick Hendrick his first NASCAR Cup title?

2. In the late 90s, Jeff Gordon's over the wall gang was known by this colorful nickname.

2. In 2004, NASCAR was featured in 3D for what large format movie theaters?

2 POINTS

3. Rick Hendrick scored his first Cup series win when what driver scored at Martinsville?

3. What driver was affectionately nicknamed 'June Bug' by his father?

3. In 2000, what famous driver placed 40th on Forbes magazines list of the 100 richest celebrities?

4. Rick went from a 2-car team to a 3-car team when he added what driver in 1987?

4. Roy Jones drove a full season for Petty Enterprises in 2001, but most race fans would know him better as what?

4. The very first live flag-to-flag television coverage of a race was what year's Daytona 500?

3 POINTS

5. When Rick Hendrick started his race team, it was originally called what?

5. This driver was known as 'Wood-chopper' before he left to become half owner of a successful team.*

5. What year did NASCAR receive cover stories in Forbes and Sports Illustrated and break 5 million in attandance for the first time?

6. What year did both Ken Schrader and Darrell Waltrip break the million dollar mark, the first for any Hendrick team?

6. What racer became known as 'Mr. September,' for winning 4 in a row in September of 1991?

6. The very first in-car camera was carried by what driver?**

Contestant	Scoring Area	TALLY

Hendrick Motorsports	Nicknames	TV, Movies & Media

1-POINT-ANSWERS

1. Tim Richmond	1. Chevrolet	1. 'Herbie, The Love Bug'
2. Jeff Gordon	2. 'Rainbow Warriors'	2. IMAX

2-POINT-ANSWERS

3. Geoffrey Bodine	3. Dale Earnhardt Jr.	3. Dale Earnhardt
4. Benny Parsons	4. 'Buckshot Jones'	4. 1979

3-POINT-ANSWERS

5. All-Star Racing	5. Glen Wood*	5. 1995
6. 1989	6. Harry Gant	6. Benny Parsons**

* Before he discovered NASCAR Glen's goal was to own and run a mill.

** BP allowed CBS to put the 80 pound camera in his car for the Daytona 500. Today cars carry three cameras weighing less than 18 pounds combined.

"The truth is not nearly as good as what the media is making up." -- Ray Evernham denying reports he was leaving Hendrick

"As soon as I got out of the car, (crew chief) Tony Eury Sr. said to me, 'Now don't cuss.' I'm glad he reminded me." -- Dale Earnhardt Jr., after winning at Phoenix

"When today's race is over, it's over. The only race that matters is the one coming up." -- Harry Gant

Roush Racing	Racing Technology	Dale Earnhardt

1 POINT

1. What driver brought Jack Roush his highest earnings for a single team in a single year?*	1. Beginning in 2002, NASCAR required teams to use the same what for qualifying, practice and race?	1. What race track did Dale Earnhardt make his NASCAR Cup debut?
2. What driver joined Roush Racing in 1996 to become Jack's third Cup team?	2. Since 2002 all over-the-wall crew are required to wear what safety device?	2. What award did Dale Earnhardt Sr. win in 1979 that Dale Jr. can never duplicate?

2 POINTS

3. Roush Racing's NEXTEL Cup teams currently call what North Carolina town home?	3. What is the pillar that runs down from the roof of the car between the windshield and the drivers window?	3. What year did Dale win 11 races in one season, including 6 of the first 8 races?
4. What year did Jack Roush enter his first NASCAR race as a car owner?	4. The soft wall technology that NASCAR tracks use is known by what brand name?	4. Dale Earnhardt won the final pole position of his NEXTEL Cup career in what year?

3 POINTS

5. Roush Industries owns what collectible and apparel manufacturer?	5. What do you call adjusting the upper and lower ball joints forward or backwards relative to each other?	5. Dale Earnhardt began his racing career in a pink car, what was the car number?
6. After a plane crash in 2002, what retired marine saved Jack's life?	6. What company is the only approved manufacturer of roof flaps?	6. When Dale Earnhardt made his NASCAR Cup debut, who was the primary sponsor on the car?

Contestant	Scoring Area	TALLY

Roush Racing	Racing Technology	Dale Earnhardt
1-POINT-ANSWERS		
1. Mark Martin*	1. Engine	1. Charlotte Motor Speedway
2. Jeff Burton	2. Helmet	2. NASCAR Cup Rookie of the Year
2-POINT-ANSWERS		
3. Concord	3. The A-post	3. 1987
4. 1988	4. SAFER Barrier System	4. 1996
3-POINT-ANSWERS		
5. Team Caliber	5. Caster	5. K-2
6. Larry Hicks	6. Roush Enterprises	6. 10,000 RPM Speed Equipment

* In 2002 Mark earned over $7 million. Contrasted with Kurt Busch's 2004 Championship season earnings which just barely cracked $4 million.

"We've got heavy hearts in the backs of our minds."
-- Kurt Busch, expressing his feelings on owner Jack Roush in the aftermath of Roush's injuries in a plane crash

"To be honest, more than likely it will take four or five guys to fill the shoes of Dale Earnhardt, if you ever can. He was our hero. But we've got this big fan base that Dale drew for us, and we've got to find a way to keep them interested in NASCAR racing." -- Dale Jarrett

Coca-Cola 600	Great Races	Race Tracks

1 POINT

1. Who is the CEO of Speedway Motorsports Inc., which owns Lowes Motor Speedway?

2. The worst start of any Coca-Cola 600 winning driver is 37th. Who overcame that deficit in 2003?

1. The last race of the year in Atlanta 1992 saw Alan Kulwicki win the Championship by only 10 points, who won the race that day?

2. What driver won the final Cup race in Rockingham, NC?

1. In 2005 the Busch Series is venturing out of the U.S. to race at what long road course?

2. How much banking is there in the corners at Talladega Superspeedway?

2 POINTS

3. In 1993, what driver claimed the Coca-Cola 600 on his way to winning the Championship that same year?

4. What year was the race that would become the Coca-Cola 600 first held?

3. In 2003, Kurt Busch lost by 0.002 seconds to who at Darlington, in the closest finish in NASCAR history?

4. The 1st Southern 500 was held at the brand new Darlington Raceway in what year?

3. What driver swept both races at Michigan International Speedway in 1985 and 1986 for four in-a-row?

4. In 1989, both races in Martinsville were swept by what driver?

3 POINTS

5. Who was the first driver to ever compete in the Indy 500 and the Coca-Cola 600 in the same year?*

6. The 1991 Coca-Cola 600 completed a sweep for what driver who won The Winston the week before?

5. Bowman-Gray Stadium hosted its final Cup race in 1971 when what driver took the checkered flag?

6. When Daytona hosted the first Bud Shootout in 1979, what driver came out on top?

5. Name the Randleman, N.C. track that hosted 3 Cup races in 1963, one of which Richard Petty won.

6. In 1958, Jim Paschal won on a paved 1/4 mile track in Asheville, N.C. called what?

Contestant	Scoring Area	TALLY

Coca-Cola 600	Great Races	Race Tracks

1-POINT-ANSWERS

Coca-Cola 600	Great Races	Race Tracks
1. O. Bruton Smith	1. Bill Elliott	1. Autodromo Hermanos Rodriguez
2. Jimmie Johnson	2. Matt Kenseth	2. 33 degrees

2-POINT-ANSWERS

Coca-Cola 600	Great Races	Race Tracks
3. Dale Earnhardt	3. Ricky Craven	3. Bill Elliott
4. 1960	4. 1950	4. Darrell Waltrip

3-POINT-ANSWERS

Coca-Cola 600	Great Races	Race Tracks
5. Cale Yarborough*	5. Bobby Allison	5. Tar Heel Speedway
6. Davey Allison	6. Buddy Baker	6. McCormick Field

* In 1967 he finished 44th on Sunday May 28th in Charlotte and then went to Indianapolis where he finished 17th in the rain delayed Indy 500 on May 30th and 31st.

"*I represent a dying breed of drivers who come from a background of racing stock cars only, who come from North Carolina and who never wanted to do anything else but drive stock cars.*" -- Scott Riggs

"*When you've fought for a car length on the track, and then have to sit through 18-20 seconds in the pits, you feel like you've lost a week.*" --Buddy Baker, on his pit crew being fast

"*We're not sure what happened to the engine, but it's obviously something internal.*" -- Greg Biffle

	Sponsors	Women In NASCAR	Drivers
1 POINT	1. After NASCAR allowed distilled spirit advertisers, what driver began the 2005 season with Jack Daniel's as a sponsor?	1. Since 2002, this female car owner has 86 starts, but only driver Ken Schader has broken into the top ten for her.	1. What opinionated driver won back-to-back 'Most Popular Driver' awards in 1989 and 1990?
	2. Both of Ricky Craven's career Cup victories came for what sponsor?	2. What woman is president of International Speedway Corp.?	2. The 2004 NEXTEL Cup 'Most Popular Driver' award went to who?
2 POINTS	3. Darrell Waltrip scored the last wins of his career in 1992 while carrying what sponsor's colors?	3. In 1994, who secured her best NASCAR result ever when she finished 10th in a Busch race at Watkins Glen?	3. Ted Musgrave's first NASCAR Cup race was in 1990, as of February 2005 how many series wins does he have?*
	4. Dale Earnhardt Jr. had what primary sponsor when he won two Busch Series Championships?	4. Boudreaux's Butt Paste sponsored who in all 5 of her 2004 Busch Series starts?	4. What year did Mark Martin start his first NASCAR Cup race?
3 POINTS	5. When Ronald Reagan arrived at Daytona International Speedway in 1984, he was wearing what sponsor's cap?	5. In 2004, what driver struggled in her 12 Busch starts, her average start and finish both above 35?	5. Crossover racing star, Dan Gurney, won three races in-a-row, from 1964-1966, at what west coast raceway?
	6. Cale Yarborough won the 1978 Championship with what sponsor?	6. What woman has five career NASCAR starts, with a best finish of 26th in Daytona in 1988?	6. This driver dominated Michigan in the 70s... winning 8 races from '72-'78.

Contestant	Scoring Area	TALLY

Sponsors	Women In NASCAR	Drivers

1-POINT-ANSWERS

Sponsors	Women In NASCAR	Drivers
1. Dave Blaney	1. Beth Ann Morgenthau	1. Darrell Waltrip
2. Tide	2. Lesa (France) Kennedy	2. Dale Earnhardt, Jr.

2-POINT-ANSWERS

Sponsors	Women In NASCAR	Drivers
3. Western Auto	3. Shawna Robinson	3. Zero*
4. AC Delco	4. Kim Crosby	4. 1981

3-POINT-ANSWERS

Sponsors	Women In NASCAR	Drivers
5. STP	5. Tina Gordon	5. Riverside International Raceway
6. 1st National City Travelers Checks	6. Patty Moise	6. David Pearson

* Ted's only NASCAR wins have come in the Craftsman Truck series where he has 15 wins in 99 starts.

"If somebody was building another Dover today and the word got out, I'd bet at least three of four drivers would chain themselves to the bulldozers in protest."
-- Kyle Petty, discussing Dover Downs

"I'm going to miss Rockingham. I wish there were more tracks like Rockingham, but that's not going to happen."
-- Ricky Rudd

Daytona 500	**Racing Families**	**Racing Teams**

1 POINT

Daytona 500

1. The 1979 race featured Cale Yarborough and Donnie Allison with a half-lap lead battling the final lap. Who won?*

2. The rain-shortened 2003 event was won by what driver?

Racing Families

1. Who is the only father/son combination to both win NASCAR's All-Star event?

2. As of February, 2005, these are the only brothers to have both won NASCAR Cup series titles.

Racing Teams

1. What driver was Bill Elliott's teammate when Ray Evernham started out as a car owner in 2001?

2. What NASCAR businessman and funnyman is the spotter for Matt Kenseth?

2 POINTS

Daytona 500

3. Who was the last driver to win back-to-back Daytona 500s?

4. What driver's 22 year (and counting) career includes only 2 wins, one of which was the 1990 Daytona 500?

Racing Families

3. What NASCAR Champion retired the same year that his son won his own Cup title?

4. In 1999 the Burton brothers finished 1-2 three times with which driver winning all three?

Racing Teams

3. When Alan Kulwicki won his NASCAR Cup title, who was his crew chief?

4. Who was Bill Elliott's crew chief when he won the NASCAR NEXTEL Cup Championship?

3 POINTS

Daytona 500

5. Richard Petty set a margin of victory record that may never be broken when he won the Daytona 500 by two full laps in what year?

6. What car make won the very first Daytona 500?

Racing Families

5. Kyle Petty became the first 3rd generation driver to win a Cup race when he won at Richmond in what year?

6. How many actual Wood brothers are there in the Wood Brothers Racing organization?**

Racing Teams

5. What car builder saw his cars win all 30 Cup races in 1978?

6. What multi-car Busch series team was the first to have all cars win and finish in the top ten in points in the same season?

Contestant	Scoring Area	TALLY

Daytona 500	Racing Families	Racing Teams

1-POINT-ANSWERS

Daytona 500	Racing Families	Racing Teams
1. Richard Petty*	1. The Earnhardts	1. Casey Atwood
2. Michael Waltrip	2. Terry and Bobby Labonte	2. Mike Calinoff

2-POINT-ANSWERS

Daytona 500	Racing Families	Racing Teams
3. Sterling Marlin	3. Lee Petty	3. Paul Andrews
4. Derrike Cope	4. Jeff	4. Ernie Elliott

3-POINT-ANSWERS

Daytona 500	Racing Families	Racing Teams
5. 1973	5. 1986	5. Banjo Matthews
6. Oldsmobile	6. 4**	6. BACE Motorsports (1998)

* Cale and Donnie wrecked in turn three, jumped out of their cars and got into a nationally televised fist fight while Petty and Darrell Waltrip battled to the flag.

** Glen and Leonard founded the team, Glen's sons Eddie and Len now run the operation.

"I came to a race and a rodeo broke out. That's all I've got to say." -- Jimmy Spencer, on the roughness of the qualifying laps at Daytona

"Second Place is just the first loser." -- Dale Earnhardt

"Make a rule a rule. That's the rule. If it's 15 yards for clipping, it's 15 yards for clipping. Whatever it is. I don't care. I just want the rule to be the same … for everybody."
-- Team owner, Ray Evernham

Richard Petty	All Star Race	Champions

1 POINT

1. Dale Inman was Richard's crew chief for all seven of his Championships plus one more with what other driver?

2. What year did Richard Petty win his first NASCAR Championship?

1. In 1998 Jeff Gordon drove a car painted with special color-changing paint called what?

2. Before 2004, the NASCAR NEXTEL All-Star Challenge was known by what sponsored name?

1. The 1991 NASCAR Cup title was claimed by what driver?

2. After Petty and Earnhardt at 7, who has the next highest number of career NASCAR Cup titles?

2 POINTS

3. There was one season where financial struggles forced Petty Enterprises to remain idle. What year was that?*

4. Richard currently lives close to Petty Enterprises in what N.C. town?

3. In 1987, Dale Earnhardt won one of the most exciting All-Star events with what famous move? †

4. The 2002 All-Star race saw what driver win it on his way to Rookie of the Year honors?

3. Name the very first Champion of what would become the NASCAR NEXTEL Cup series.

4. What NASCAR Cup Champion scored his first career series victory at Bristol in the spring of 2002?

3 POINTS

5. After Richard retired from driving, what driver first took over the STP car?

6. In '92, President George Bush gave Richard what award for distinguished civilian performance in peacetime?

5. What driver won the very first All-Star race?

6. Of Jeff Gordon's four Championships, how many times did he also win the All-Star race in the same year?

5. Who was the first driver to win back-to-back Cup Championships?

6. 2002 Champ, Tony Stewart, has never had a NASCAR Cup season without a win. His first win came at what race track in 1999?

Contestant	Scoring Area	TALLY

Richard Petty   All Star Race   Champions

1-POINT-ANSWERS

Richard Petty	All Star Race	Champions
1. Terry Labonte	1. Chromalusion	1. Dale Earnhardt
2. 1964	2. 'The Winston'	2. Jeff Gordon - 4

2-POINT-ANSWERS

Richard Petty	All Star Race	Champions
3. 1985*	3. 'The Pass In The Grass'†	3. Red Byron
4. Level Cross	4. Ryan Newman	4. Kurt Busch

3-POINT-ANSWERS

Richard Petty	All Star Race	Champions
5. Rick Wilson	5. Darrell Waltrip	5. Buck Baker
6. Presidential Medal of Freedom	6. Three	6. Richmond International Raceway

* Richard drove for car owner Mike Curb and Kyle landed a ride with the Wood Brothers. Richard returned to PE in 1986.

† Technically it was not a pass. Bill Elliott hit Earnhardt in the back and he skittered across the grass and back onto the track, maintaining his lead.

"Another big deal was in 1992, when I went to the White House to receive the Medal of Freedom from President Bush... It was a big day for (my wife) Lynda and me. I probably wouldn't have gone to the ceremony if Clinton had called me up there." -- Richard Petty

"Once he understands how something works, he goes out and masters it. Kurt, once he makes a mistake, dedicates himself to rectifying it, and that's a remarkable attribute in a young man." -- Jack Roush, on Kurt Busch

	Rookies	Race Tracks	Nicknames
1 POINT	1. Tony Stewart and Jimmie Johnson share the record for NASCAR Cup wins by a rookie with how many?	1. Rusty Wallace took the very first NASCAR Cup victory when what track opened in 1993?	1. What difficult to master oval on the NASCAR Cup schedule is 'The Track Too Tough To Tame?'
	2. What driver beat Dale Earnhardt Jr for 'Rookie of the Year' honors in 2000?	2. Which of the NASCAR Cup race tracks bills itself as a 1.54 mile quad-oval?	2. 'The Great American Race' is the nickname for what prestigous NASCAR event?
2 POINTS	3. In 1989 Rusty Wallace claimed the title while what driver with the unfortunate name won Rookie of the Year?	3. The Busch and Truck series both visit what 1.0 mile track with 9.25 degrees of banking?	3. Dale Earnhardt was the owner of the Kannapolis baseball team that changed their nickname to what?
	4. Which award is older Rookie of the Year or Most Popular Driver?*	4. What year did Texas Motor Speedway first host NEXTEL Cup competition?	4. What driver's DVD biography is named "Smoke" after his NASCAR nickname?
3 POINTS	5. What 1983 NASCAR Cup 'Rookie of the Year' didn't score his first series win until the 1994 Daytona 500?	5. What former NASCAR track went under the wrecking ball after Rusty Wallace won its June 1988 race?	5. 'Suitcase Jake' was the crew chief for David Pearson's 1968 and 1969 Championships. Jake who?
	6. What driver won the 1982 NASCAR Cup 'Rookie of the Year' honors?	6. Who won the very first NASCAR Cup race at Phoenix International Raceway?	6. What driver, who never won a Championship, was the original 'Golden Boy' of NASCAR?

Contestant	Scoring Area	TALLY

Rookies	Race Tracks	Nicknames

1-POINT-ANSWERS

Rookies	Race Tracks	Nicknames
1. Three	1. New Hampshire Intrernational Speedway	1. Darlington Raceway
2. Matt Kenseth	2. Atlanta Motor Speedway	2. Daytona 500

2-POINT-ANSWERS

Rookies	Race Tracks	Nicknames
3. Dick Trickle	3. The Milwaukee Mile	3. 'The Intimidators'
4. Most Popular Driver*	4. 1997	4. Tony Stewart

3-POINT-ANSWERS

Rookies	Race Tracks	Nicknames
5. Sterling Marlin	5. Riverside International Raceway	5. Elder
6. Geoffrey Bodine	6. Alan Kulwicki	6. Fred Lorenzen

* 'Most Popular Driver' was first awarded in 1956, while 'Rookie of the Year' was first given in 1958.

"I got in the ambulance and looked back over there and I said 'Man, the wheels ain't knocked off that car yet... Get out. I gotta go.'" -- Dale Earnhardt, 1997

"Brendan Gaughan came over, and he said, 'I can't believe you've got a special paint scheme your first race.'" -- Carl Edwards, debuting in Cup at Michigan.

"You know, I can't stand over-optimistic people." -- Mark Martin

Dale Earnhardt	Jeff Gordon	Racing History
1 POINT		
1. Dale Earnhardt loved Bristol. Who did he punt across the finish line (and finish second to) in August of 1995?*	1. What year did Jeff Gordon win his first NASCAR Cup series points-paying race?	1. NASCAR's first blockbuster event was their first 500 miler which came at what new track in 1950?
2. What was Dale Earnhardt's father's first name?	2. Jeff Gordon ran the full Busch series schedule in 1992 with what primary sponsor?	2. Many of NASCAR's early drivers learned their skills in what occupation?
2 POINTS		
3. Who was the first full-time driver hired to drive for Dale Earnhardt Incorporated?	3. Jeff Gordon hit the big time in 2003 when he hosted what live television show?	3. What is the only original 1949 race track still on the NASCAR NEXTEL Cup schedule today?
4. Four of Dale's Championships came with what legendary crew chief behind him?	4. What year did Ray Evernham first go to work as Jeff Gordon's crew chief?	4. When the series (now known as NEXTEL Cup) debuted, what was it then called?
3 POINTS		
5. Who was the car owner that gave Dale Earnhardt his first NASCAR Cup start?	5. Jeff Gordon was born in what California town?	5. The first road race in NASCAR history was in 1954 when Al Keller won at what New Jersey track?
6. At Richard Childress' urging, who was Dale Earnhardt car owner in 1982 and 1983?	6. What driver did Jeff Gordon bump out of the way at Darlington to claim The Winston Million?	6. What car owner won the very first NASCAR Cup Championship?

Contestant	Scoring Area	TALLY

Dale Earnhardt	**Jeff Gordon**	**Racing History**

1-POINT-ANSWERS

Dale Earnhardt	Jeff Gordon	Racing History
1. Terry Labonte*	1. 1994	1. Darlington Raceway
2. Ralph	2. Baby Ruth	2. Bootlegger (Moonshiner)

2-POINT-ANSWERS

Dale Earnhardt	Jeff Gordon	Racing History
3. Steve Park	3. Saturday Night Live	3. Martinsville Speedway
4. Kirk Shelmerdine	4. 1992	4. Strictly Stock

3-POINT-ANSWERS

Dale Earnhardt	Jeff Gordon	Racing History
5. Ed Negre	5. Vallejo, California	5. Linden Airport
6. Bud Moore	6. Jeff Burton	6. Raymond Parks

* In a much more famous incident four years later, Earnhardt won the 1999 race by again wrecking Terry Labonte on the last lap.

"Stock car racing never would have started if the Government hadn't chosen to Tax Moonshine." -- Curtis Turner

NOTE: Curtis Turner and many of the pioneer drivers of NASCAR built their first cars to out run revenue agents while hauling White Lightening. Turner once demonstrated the bootleg turn (where a car spins 180 degrees to get it headed in the opposite direction) to a skeptical West Coast writer on a Los Angeles freeway. A State Trooper pulled him over and became intrigued by the story, so Turner demonstrated the bootleg turn for him as well.

Busch Series	Manufacturers	IROC

1 POINT

1. What is the Busch series team called that Dale Earnhardt Jr and Theresa Earnhardt own?

1. Ford has raced the Taurus in NASCAR since 1998. Before the Taurus, what model did the Ford teams use?

1. From 1994 through 2000, what driver never finished worse than second in the final IROC standings?

2. What driver scored back-to-back Busch series Championships in 1996 and 1997?

2. In 2004. which car maker claimed the NEXTEL Cup manufacturers title?

2. The 1993, IROC title was won by what driver after his death?*

2 POINTS

3. What Busch series great scored his first series victory at Lanier Speedway in 1991?

3. When Dale Earnhardt won his first title he drove Chevys, except for three races where he drove what make instead?**

3. In 1999, Mark Martin missed out on winning the IROC Championship by just one point when what driver narrowly beat him?

4. Kyle Busch won his first NASCAR Busch Series race in 2004 at what race track?

4. The 1963 season saw Mercury enter NASCAR with what model?

4. In 2001, what was the shortest track on the IROC Schedule?

3 POINTS

5. As of 2/05, what 55-time NASCAR Cup race winner has never won a Busch series race in 36 tries over 8 seasons?

5. What manufacturer is credited with winning the first NASCAR Cup event?

5. What driver won his only IROC Championship in 1984, beating Neil Bonnett and Darrell Waltrip for the title?

6. In 1983-84, this driver became the first back-to-back Busch series Champ.

6. What year did Pontiac win its final NEXTEL Cup manufacturers title?

6. In 1976, what driver won the IROC title without ever winning a race?

Contestant	Scoring Area	TALLY

Busch Series   Manufacturers   IROC

1-POINT-ANSWERS

1. Chance 2 Motorsports	1. Thunderbird	1. Mark Martin
2. Randy Lajoie	2. Chevrolet	2. Davey Allison*

2-POINT-ANSWERS

3. David Green	3. Oldsmobile**	3. Dale Earnhardt
4. Richmond	4. Marauder	4. Michigan International Speedway

3-POINT-ANSWERS

5. Rusty Wallace	5. Lincoln	5. Cale Yarborough
6. Sam Ard	6. 1993	6. AJ Foyt

* Terry Labonte filled in for Davey for the final race and the $175,000 prize money was donated to a trust fund for Davey's children.

** At the Daytona 500 and both Talladega races, Earnhardt switched to Oldsmobile. With Olds, Dale finished 4th, 2nd and 3rd in those three races.

"There is only one lap you want to lead, and that's the last lap." -- Ralph Earnhardt's advice to his son Dale

"The problem is you've got a young kid who is trying to replace Dale Earnhardt, who thinks he is Dale Earnhardt, and right now he wouldn't be a scab on Dale Earnhardt's butt." -- Bobby Hamilton, on then rookie, Kevin Harvick

"For five minutes, I felt like my daddy."
-- Dale Earnhardt Jr., after winning at Richmond

	Racing Rules	**Drivers**	**Great Races**
1 POINT	1. What is the penalty for missing the NASCAR drivers' meeting? 2. At Bristol in 2004, what driver was fined $10,000 and 25 points for intentionally spinning himself out?	1. From 1990 - 1999, what driver lead all NASCAR Cup competitors in road course victories?* 2. This 2004 driver won three NEXTEL Cup races in a row during October.	1. From 1985 until 1997, winning 3 out of 4 of NASCAR's First, Fastest, Longest and Oldest races would collect what bonus program? 2. What driver won the last Cup race of the 90s?
2 POINTS	3. How many crew members are allowed to go over the wall during a pitstop? 4. What color is the 'move over' flag that tells slower drivers that the leaders are behind them?	3. What driver was the first to score wins in all three of NASCAR's top (Cup, Busch and Truck) series? 4. What independent racer flipped his only race car at Rockingham in February of 2004?	3. In 2001, what driver won at Rockingham, the first race after Dale Earnhardt passed away? 4. Who won the first NASCAR exhibition race on the road course in Suzuka, Japan?
3 POINTS	5. How many points does the leader get when the top 10 drivers are locked in with 10 races to go? 6. The penalty for speeding while entering pit road is to be held in your pit stall for how long?	5. What driver became the first back-to-back winner in Talladega history when he swept both races in 1970? 6. What NASCAR legend had a record 11 consecutive poles at Lowes Motor Speedway?	5. In 1961, who won the pole for the first race ever at Bristol Motor Speedway with a blistering lap of 79.225 mph? 6. In 1963, he won the only caution-free Southern 500 in history.

Contestant	Scoring Area	TALLY

Racing Rules   Drivers   Great Races

1-POINT-ANSWERS

Racing Rules	Drivers	Great Races
1. Start at the back of the pack	1. Jeff Gordon*	1. The Winston Million
2. Dale Earnhardt Jr.	2. Jimmie Johnson	2. Bobby Labonte

2-POINT-ANSWERS

Racing Rules	Drivers	Great Races
3. Seven	3. Kenny Schrader	3. Steve Park
4. Blue with an orange diagonal stripe	4. Carl Long	4. Rusty Wallace

3-POINT-ANSWERS

Racing Rules	Drivers	Great Races
5. 5,050	5. Pete Hamilton	5. Fred Lorenzen
6. 15 seconds	6. David Pearson	6. Fireball Roberts

* Jeff Gordon had 5, Mark Martin 4, Ernie Irvan 3, Rusty Wallace and Geoffrey Bodine tied at 2 while four others each had one.

"I guess it (the Busch championship) will sink in once I see my daddy's eyes next week." -- Dale Earnhardt Jr., 1998

"I'd say he definitely had the better car and he was probably going to win the race. I killed his chances of doing that." -- Dale Earnhardt, Jr, on his wreck with Matt Kenseth

"Don't hit him! I know you can hear me, and NASCAR said that they are watching you."-- Ty Norris, trying to talk Dale Earnhardt, Jr out of hitting Kurt Busch after Busch had wrecked the #8 earlier. *"You're breaking up man. I still can't hear you."* -- Dale Earnhardt, Jr's reply

Racing Technology	Race Tracks	TV, Movies & Media
1 POINT		
1. Tires that were run for a couple of laps and allowed to cool before being raced are called what?	1. What Cup series track is listed at 1.058 miles in length with 12 degrees of banking?	1. In 2004, ESPN released "3," a full-length TV movie about the life of what NASCAR star?
2. The fireproof material that the driver's suit and underwear are made of is called what?	2. What tricky triangle is 'the superspeedway that drives like a road course?'	2. The weekly NASCAR bible, 'NASCAR Scene,' was known by what name prior to the 2004 season?
2 POINTS		
3. Hard rubber that is inserted into the coils of a spring to adjust the handling is called what?	3. Better known for football, what venue saw Fireball Roberts win a 200 lapper in 1956?	3. In 1977, Richard Pryor starred in a true-life movie about what African American stock car driver?
4. What is the pillar that runs down from the roof of the car beside the rear window?	4. What west coast track held its first NASCAR Cup race in 1988?	4. What year did Fox, NBC and their related channels take over NASCAR TV coverage?
3 POINTS		
5. What year did Goodyear introduce the inner-liner as a significant safety feature for its racing tires?	5. Parnelli Jones won a NASCAR road course race in 1957 at Kitsap County Airport in what state?	5. Who founded MRN, because he didn't think that traditional media was doing a good job covering NASCAR?
6. NASCAR teams put what kind of gas in their tires instead of regular old air?	6. What year did the total purse for the cup race in Michigan first exceed $1 million?	6. The very first time NASCAR was seen on TV was a clip of what race in 1961?

Contestant	Scoring Area	TALLY

Racing Technology	Race Tracks	TV, Movies & Media

1-POINT-ANSWERS

Racing Technology	Race Tracks	TV, Movies & Media
1. Scuffs	1. New Hampshire International Speedway	1. Dale Earnhardt
2. Nomex or Proban	2. Pocono Raceway	2. 'Winston Cup Scene'

2-POINT-ANSWERS

Racing Technology	Race Tracks	TV, Movies & Media
3. Spring rubber	3. Soldier Field	3. Wendell Scott
4. The C-post	4. Phoenix International Raceway	4. 2001

3-POINT-ANSWERS

Racing Technology	Race Tracks	TV, Movies & Media
5. 1964	5. Washington	5. Bill France, Sr.
6. Nitrogen	6. 1996	6. Firecracker (Pepsi) 400

From the movie... "Days of Thunder" (1990)

Cole Trickle: *"Yeah, well the sonofabitch just slammed into me."* Harry Hogge: *"No, no, he didn't slam into you, he didn't bump you, he didn't nudge you... he RUBBED you. And rubbin', son, is racin'."*

"Control is an illusion, you infantile egomaniac. Nobody knows what's gonna happen next: not on a freeway, not in an airplane, not inside our own bodies and certainly not on a racetrack with 40 other infantile egomaniacs."
-- Dr. Claire Lewicki, from 'Days of Thunder'

	Drivers	Craftsman Truck Series	Sponsors
1 POINT	1. What driver with 15 Busch series starts, and 0 top tens, watched his son win the 2004 Busch title?	1. What manufacturer entered the Craftsman Truck Series in 2004, with trucks built in its Costa Mesa, California facility?	1. Prior to 1998, the Bud Shootout trophy dash for the previous year's pole winners was known as what race?
	2. What NASCAR star hails from Batesville, Arkansas?	2. In 1998, what driver became the first 2-time Truck Series Champion?	2. Dale Jarrett won the Championship carrying the colors for what sponsor?
2 POINTS	3. When Kyle Petty won the first NASCAR Cup race of his career, what number was his 7-Eleven sponsored car?	3. What driver took the 2002 Craftsman Truck Series Championship?	3. In 2004, Jimmie Johnson was fined for offending what company that provides the official sports beverage of NASCAR?
	4. Who was the only driver to score his only NASCAR Cup victory in 2002?	4. With a 14th place points finish, what driver scored the 2004 Craftsman Truck Series Rookie of the Year award?	4. Before 1986, the Coca-Cola 600 was known by this unsponsored name.
3 POINTS	5. What driver's final NASCAR Cup victory came in Atlanta, while driving the famous #21 Wood Brothers' Citgo Ford?	5. What future NASCAR star was only 16 when he made his truck series debut at IRP in 2001?	5. Kyle Petty scored his first career win in 1986 with what sponsor on the hood?
	6. The final win of his career came in Richmond, in the spring of 1993, for what driver?	6. What driver won the first superspeedway race in truck series history when won Daytona in 2000?	6. Terry Labonte scored his first NASCAR Cup win in 1980 with what primary sponsor?

Contestant	Scoring Area	TALLY

Craftsman Truck Series

Drivers	Truck Series	Sponsors

1-POINT-ANSWERS

Drivers	Craftsman Truck Series	Sponsors
1. Martin Truex	1. Toyota	1. Busch Clash
2. Mark Martin	2. Ron Hornaday, Jr.	2. Quality Care / Ford Credit

2-POINT-ANSWERS

Drivers	Craftsman Truck Series	Sponsors
3. 7	3. Mike Bliss	3. Powerade
4. Johnny Benson, Jr.	4. David Reutimann	4. World 600

3-POINT-ANSWERS

Drivers	Craftsman Truck Series	Sponsors
5. Morgan Shepherd	5. Kyle Busch	5. 7-Eleven
6. Davey Allison	6. Mike Wallace	6. Apache Classic Stove

"You can tell that you're in trouble when you feel the air on the back of your neck instead of in your face."
-- Buddy Baker

"What makes the Monte Carlo so good? ME!"
-- Dale Earnhardt

"They're going to have to come in here and bulldoze the place." -- Rusty Wallace, complaining about New Hampshire International Speedway

"I told Joe a month ago that winning is like sex. The more you do it, the more you like it." -- Felix Sabates

NASCAR Champions

Year	Champion	Car Owner
2006	_____	_____
2005		
	_____	_____
2004	Kurt Busch	Jack Roush
2003	Matt Kenseth	Jack Roush
2002	Tony Stewart	Joe Gibbs
2001	Jeff Gordon	Rick Hendrick
2000	Bobby Labonte	Joe Gibbs
1999	Dale Jarrett	Robert Yates
1998	Jeff Gordon	Rick Hendrick
1997	Jeff Gordon	Rick Hendrick
1996	Terry Labonte	Rick Hendrick
1995	Jeff Gordon	Rick Hendrick
1994	Dale Earnhardt	Richard Childress
1993	Dale Earnhardt	Richard Childress
1992	Alan Kulwicki	Alan Kulwicki
1991	Dale Earnhardt	Richard Childress
1990	Dale Earnhardt	Richard Childress
1989	Rusty Wallace	Raymond Beadle
1988	Bill Elliott	Harry Melling
1987	Dale Earnhardt	Richard Childress
1986	Dale Earnhardt	Richard Childress
1985	Darrell Waltrip	Junior Johnson
1984	Terry Labonte	Billy Hagan
1983	Bobby Allison	Bill Gardner
1982	Darrell Waltrip	Junior Johnson
1981	Darrell Waltrip	Junior Johnson
1980	Dale Earnhardt	Rod Osterlund
1979	Richard Petty	Petty Enterprises
1978	Cale Yarborough	Junior Johnson
1977	Cale Yarborough	Junior Johnson
1976	Cale Yarborough	Junior Johnson
1975	Richard Petty	Petty Enterprises
1974	Richard Petty	Petty Enterprises
1973	Benny Parsons	L.G. DeWitt
1972	Richard Petty	Petty Enterprises
1971	Richard Petty	Petty Enterprises
1970	Bobby Isaac	Nord Krauskopf
1969	David Pearson	Holman-Moody
1968	David Pearson	Holman-Moody
1967	Richard Petty	Petty Enterprises
1966	David Pearson	Cotton Owens
1965	Ned Jarrett	Bondy Long
1964	Richard Petty	Petty Enterprises
1963	Joe Weatherly	Bud Moore
1962	Joe Weatherly	Bud Moore
1961	Ned Jarrett	B.G. Holloway
1960	Rex White	White-Clements

1959	Lee Petty	Petty Enterprises
1958	Lee Petty	Petty Enterprises
1957	Buck Baker	Buck Baker
1956	Buck Baker	Carl Kiekhaefer
1955	Tim Flock	Carl Kiekhaefer
1954	Lee Petty	Petty Enterprises
1953	Herb Thomas	Herb Thomas
1952	Tim Flock	Ted Chester
1951	Herb Thomas	Herb Thomas
1950	Bill Rexford	Julian Buesink
1949	Red Byron	Raymond Parks

Busch Series Champions

Year	Champion	Car Owner
2004	Martin Truex Jr.	Dale Earnhardt Inc.
2003	Brian Vickers	Ricky Hendrick
2002	Greg Biffle	Jack Roush
2001	Kevin Harvick	Dale Earnhardt Inc.
2000	Jeff Green	Greg Pollex
1999	Dale Earnhardt Jr.	Dale Earnhardt Inc.
1998	Dale Earnhardt Jr.	Dale Earnhardt Inc.
1997	Randy LaJoie	Bill Baumgardner
1996	Randy LaJoie	Bill Baumgardner
1995	Johnny Benson Jr.	Bill Baumgardner
1994	David Green	Bob Labonte
1993	Steve Grissom	Wayne Grissom
1992	Joe Nemechek	Joe Nemechek
1991	Bobby Labonte	Bob Labonte
1990	Chuck Bown	Hubert Hensley
1989	Rob Moroso	Dick Moroso
1988	Tommy Ellis	John Jackson
1987	Larry Pearson	David Pearson
1986	Larry Pearson	David Pearson
1985	Jack Ingram	Jack Ingram
1984	Sam Ard	Howard Thomas
1983	Sam Ard	Howard Thomas
1982	Jack Ingram	Jack Ingram

Craftsman Truck Series Champions

Year	Champion	Truck Owner
2004	Bobby Hamilton	Bobby Hamilton
2003	Travis Kvapil	Steve Coulter
2002	Mike Bliss	Steve Coulter
2001	Jack Sprague	Rick Hendrick
2000	Greg Biffle	Jack Roush
1999	Jack Sprague	Rick Hendrick
1998	Ron Hornaday, Jr.	Dale Earnhardt Inc.
1997	Jack Sprague	Rick Hendrick
1996	Ron Hornaday, Jr.	Dale Earnhardt Inc.
1995	Mike Skinner	Richard Childress

Stock Car Racing GLOSSARY

Stock Car Racing has a language all its own. Following is a list of terms you might hear around any NASCAR garage.

AERO PUSH – When closely following another car, the lead car prevents the air from hitting the nose of the second car. There is less downforce on the front of the trailing vehicle and it does not turn as well resulting in aero push.

AERODYNAMIC DRAG – See DRAG

AIR DAM – The front air dam is the strip of metal that hangs on the nose of the car below the front grill. Teams adjust the air dam and ride height to get this as close as possible to the ground preventing air from getting under the car which would decrease downforce.

AIR PRESSURE – A change in air pressure affects many aspects of the cars handling. The size of the tires contact patch with the track can be changed as well as the effective spring rate of that corner of the car. Adding air to the front tires would make the front stiffer and decrease those tires' grip, causing the car to feel tighter.

BACK MARKER – A slower car, usually about to be lapped by the leaders.

BALANCE – Balance describes the looseness or tightness of the car. If the car is in perfect balance all four tires would break loose at the same time. If the front breaks loose first the car is tight, if the back breaks loose first the car would be loose. The ideal state is perfect balance.

BANKING – The angle of the race track compared to level. For example the turns in Daytona are banked at 31 degrees while Martinsville features only 12 degrees.

CAMBER – Camber is the angle at which a tire makes contact with the track. Positive means that the top of the tire is tipped out while negative indicates that the top of the tire is tipped inwards. NASCAR drivers normally run positive camber in the left front and negative camber in the right front to help the car turn on the track banking.

CHASSIS – The roll cage and frame of the car. The chassis provides the core of the car that all suspension and body parts are attached to.

CHASSIS ROLL – The tendancy of the car to lean towards the outside of the turn. A softer suspension will give more chassis roll, while a stiffer suspension will keep the car from rolling as much.

CONTACT PATCH – The part of the tire that touches the track.

DIRTY AIR – As one car moves through the air it causes the air to tumble and spin beside and behind it. This dirty air does not provide good downforce for another car driving through it and can even upset the handling of another car.

DOWNFORCE – When air passes over the car it pushes back and down. Downforce is the downward component of that force and it helps the car stick to the track. Increasing downforce also increases drag, which slows straightaway speeds.

DRAFT – When a car travels through the air it leaves a gap behind it. Another car driving in this gap doesn't have as much air resistance pushing on it's nose and can then travel faster or use less fuel to travel the same speed. This effect can be noticed at speeds as low as 70mph but the effect increases with speed.

DRAG – When air passes over the car it pushes both back and down. Drag is the backwards component of that force. Drag acts against the engine's effort to push the car forwards.

ENGINE BLOCK – The solid portion of the engine which has the pistons, crank shaft and valve covers attached to it.

FABRICATOR – The person who specializes in forming sheet metal to create the body of the race car.

FIREWALL – A solid metal plate that separates the engine compartment from the cockpit of the race car.

FRONT CLIP – The part of the car from the front edge of the rollcage forwards to the front bumper. This includes the frame, suspension components and motor mounts.

FUEL CELL – The gas tank. On a NASCAR NEXTEL Cup race car it holds 22 gallons of fuel and includes numerous safety features to prevent fuel spillage during an accident.

GROOVE – The line that the majority of drivers use around the track. Often you can actually see the groove in the corners as the cars leave a little bit of rubber on the track. Depending on changing track and weather conditions the location of the groove can change during the race.

HAPPY HOUR – Slang term for the last official practice session held before a race. This usually takes place the day before the event and after all qualifying and support races have been staged.

HANDLING – The overall description of how a car drives. Usually described in terms of loose and tight at various places around the track. Suspension, aerodynamics, tires and other cars all affect the handling at any given moment.

INTERVAL – The gap between two cars often described in car lengths, yards or in time behind.

LAPPED TRAFFIC – Any car that is one or more laps behind the leader. See back marker.

LOOSE – This is when the front tires are getting a better grip on the racetrack than the rear tires. This causes the back end to want to come around in the turns making the nose of the car point towards the inside of the corner. A car that is set up to be a little bit loose is generally faster.

MARBLES – Pieces of the tires that have been ground off of the cars and have bounced up just out of the groove. There is significantly less traction "in the marbles."

NEUTRAL – When a car is neither loose nor tight.

OVERSTEER – See LOOSE

PANHARD BAR – See TRACK BAR

PIT ROAD – Portion of the track where in-race service takes place. This is normally found on the inside of the track along the front stretch, sometimes separated from the racing surface by a wall, sometimes just by grass.

PIT STALL – The specific portion of pit road allocated to a team for the race. Pit stalls are chosen by teams based on their qualifying results.

POLE POSITION – The number one qualified car. On oval courses this is the left side of the front row so as to have the preferred inside lane in the first turn.

PUSH – See TIGHT

QUARTER PANEL – The body of the car surrounding the wheels. From the bumper to where the car door would be is the quarter panel.

REAR CLIP – The part of the car from the back edge of the rollcage back to the rear bumper. This includes the frame, suspension components and trunk.

RESTRICTOR PLATE – A flat aluminum square put between the carborator and the intake manifold with holes drilled in it designed to limit the amount of air that enters the engine. This effectively limits the horsepower of the engine and slows the cars down.

ROOF FLAPS – Parts embedded in the roof of the car designed to pop up when the car travels backwards and help keep the car on the ground. These flaps disturb the aerodynamic lift that a race car generates when going backwards at high speeds.

ROUND – The standard unit of measurement for wedge and track bar adjustments. These adjustments are made by sticking a wrench into a hole in the back window and turning a bolt. One full 360 degree turn of the bolt is one round.

SETUP – The current setting of all adjustable components of the car. This includes suspension, air pressure, spoiler angles and anything else that can be changed on the car.

SHORT TRACK – Race track that is less than one mile in length.

SILLY SEASON – The off track driver, sponsor and team changes that happen during the NASCAR season.

SPOILER – The rear wing of the car. This sticks up from the far back edge of the trunk and its angle can be adjusted to affect the handling of the car.

STAGGER – The difference in circumference between the left- and right-side tires. Not as much of a setup factor since the introduction of radial tires.

STICK – Slang term used for tire traction.

STICKERS – Tires that are brand new.

STOP 'N' GO – A penalty in which the driver has to come down pit road and come to a full stop in his pit stall before returning to competition.

SUPERSPEEDWAY – NASCAR officially defines any track greater than one mile in length as a superspeedway. More commonly, a sperspeedway is any track greater than two miles in length.

SWAY BAR – Sometimes called an "antiroll bar." Bar used to resist or counteract the rolling force of the car body through the turns.

TEMPLATE – The metal outline that NASCAR officials place against the car to see if it meets the rules.

TIGHT – This is when the front tires are not getting enough grip on the racetrack. This causes the car to want to continue straight ahead when the driver turns the wheel. This is the opposite of loose.

TOE – How much the front tires on the race car point towards or away from each other. Oval cars typically run negative toe such that the two front tires are pointed in towards each other slightly.

TRACK BAR – This attaches the frame to the rear suspension and can be raised or lowered to alter the handling of the race car.

Stock Car Racing Glossary CONTINUED

TRAILING ARM – Part of the suspension with holds the rear axle in place while allowing it to travel up and down over bumps.

TRI-OVAL – A race track with a bend in the front stretch but a straight back stretch. Lowes Motor Speedway is the classic example of a tri-oval.

TURBULANCE – See DIRTY AIR

UNDERSTEER – See TIGHT

VALANCE – See AIR DAM

VICTORY LANE – The place where the winner of the race goes to celebrate, speak with the press and take numerous photos. Also called the winners circle.

WEDGE – The adjustment of the relative weight of diagonal corners of the car. This is done by preloading the springs in the rear of the car to shift more weight to, or from the opposite corner of the car. A wedge adjustment compresses or releases the spring on that side of the rear suspension.

WEIGHT JACKING – See WEDGE

WIND TUNNEL – A room with a large fan that can simulate wind blowing at race speeds. These rooms have high tech measuring devices that can determine the amount of downforce and drag that the car has. This testing is invaluable to teams who can make small changes and measure their effect precisely without the other variables present at the race track.

OTHER NOTES

_____

_____

_____

_____

_____

_____

_____

_____

_____

Thanks for playing 'YaKnow Stock Car Racing.'
Visit www.yaknowtrivia.com soon to see other popular pocket-size trivia gamebooks for reading fun on the run.